SPLITTING THE MIDDLE

SPLITTING THE MIDDLE

Political Alienation, Acquiescence, and Activism Among America's Middle Layers

CEDRIC HERRING

PRAEGER

New York
Westport, Connecticut
London

Library of Congress Cataloging-in-Publication Data

Herring, Cedric.
    Splitting the middle : political alienation, acquiescence, and
activism among America's middle layers / Cedric Herring.
      p.   cm.
    Bibliography: p.
    Includes index.
    ISBN 0–275–93321–0 (alk. paper)
    1. Political participation—United States. 2. Political
socialization—United States. 3. Middle classes—United States—
Political activity. 4. Capitalism—United States.   I. Title.
JK1764.H47   1989
323'.042'0973—dc20   89–16080

Library of Congress Catalog Card Number: 89–16080
ISBN: 0–275–93321–0

First published in 1989

Praeger Publishers, One Madison Avenue, New York, NY 10010
A division of Greenwood Press, Inc.

Printed in the United States of America

The paper used in this book complies with the
Permanent Paper Standard issued by the National
Information Standards Organization (Z39.48–1984).

10 9 8 7 6 5 4 3 2 1

In loving memory of my daughter,
Corrine Mariel Herring,
and my father,
Curtis O. Herring, Sr.
Your loving spirits will be
my inspiration always.

Contents

Contents

Tables and Figures

Acknowledgments

This work would not have been possible without the advice, guidance, and support of many important actors. I owe a great deal of thanks to Michael Schwartz, who read and commented on this manuscript. His comments and suggestions were invaluable. Others who have read and commented on parts of various drafts include Aldon Morris, Jim House, Jim Burk, Ben Aguirre, and Joe Feagin. Their input has improved my arguments, and it has forced me to make some of my points more clearly. For the remaining shortcomings, however, I take full responsibility.

An endeavor such as this is made less overwhelming with the love and support of a caring family. My wife, Marsha Church Herring, bore the brunt of my frustrations with completing data analysis and manuscript preparation tasks. I owe a great debt of gratitude to her for her patience and love. I also thank other members of my family for that special support that only they could give.

The research undertaken here was made possible by the generous financial support that I received from the National Science Foundation, the Ford Foundation, and Texas A&M University. I would also like to extend a special thanks to my Department Head, Mary Zey, for allowing me to take a leave so that I might finish the writing and rewriting.

Introduction

Since the mid 1960s, America's political institutions have suffered dramatic declines in the levels of trust and confidence granted to them. These declines have a class basis and reflect varying degrees of disappointment with the class-biased policies of the state. In particular, during the relatively unique circumstances of the 1960s and 1970s, social movement activists successfully challenged the prerogatives of policymakers and state managers. Consequently, these policymakers, who ordinarily act to guarantee the conditions necessary for profitmaking, were hindered in their attempts to secure the abeyance of noncapitalists. They bolstered the state's flagging support and forestalled a legitimacy crisis by acceeding to the demands of underdog groups, expanding social welfare programs, increasing the citizen wage, and allowing more groups to have input into the political process. These actions, aimed at appeasing progressive activists and their allies who posed serious threats to the operation of the capitalist system, were quite successful during periods of economic expansion and growth.

As economic recessions became more frequent and severe, however, state managers chose to pursue policies geared toward restarting the engine of industry at the expense of middle-layer workers. They began to use high levels of unemployment to discipline not only traditional workers, but also professionals and managers. In addition, they started cutting back on programs for the middle layers as well as for the poor. Policymakers began redirecting state funds away from social programs and toward subsidies to industry. The citizen wage was cut, and the tax burden was redistributed to the middle layers. Because social movements had begun to demobilize and were relying more on professional reform efforts, such options became more available to state managers who sought to bring about "economic growth," but levels of political alienation among noncapitalists climbed precipitously.

Policies aimed at expanding business activity also had the effect of splitting the middle. On the one hand, the social movements of the 1960s and 1970s had exposed millions of members of the middle layers to the capitalist biases of the state. These people were already prone to antigovernment sentiments. Many of them already felt that political leaders were not responsive to their needs and interests. When large proportions of them were plunged into economic despondency, they became more concerned about their personal economic security, and their levels of political alienation soared higher.

On the other hand, a more conservative element of the middle layers had experienced high levels of political alienation during the height of the movement activities. They had seen political leaders as ineffectual and too willing to pander to the whims of blacks, feminists, militants, and other "un-American" elements. Inasmuch as they went virtually unscathed by the economic policies of the state, they more readily identified with corporate and business interests. They were far more concerned with reducing the size of government and decreasing their tax burden than they were with issues of equity.

Clearly, the events of the 1960s and 1970s did not affect members of the society in the same fashion. Nor did these occurrences have the same effects on those in the middle layers. Indeed, as the expansion of direct democratic participation (in the form of social movement activity and other kinds of collective action) weakened the authority of the state, the middle layers became polarized. They were not uniform in their levels of class consciousness and their support for the different causes of the era. Even the shrinking economy of the period led to greater polarization of the middle layers, as people were differentially affected and, therefore, had substantially different views about the appropriateness of the steps the state took. Vacillation by state managers led to high levels of alienation for all members of the middle layers.

In putting forth this argument, *Splitting the Middle* demonstrates the limitations of existing attempts to account for the dramatic increases in political alienation. It argues and documents that "spirit of the times" explanations—that is, those claiming that increases in political alienation reflect such events as the Vietnam War and the Watergate scandal, which supposedly affected the entire U.S. population in a similar fashion—are inaccurate. It also shows that "political socialization and culture" theories, though extremely popular in both mainstream political science and sociology, cannot account for the trends in political alienation because these formulations do not accurately gauge the amount of change that has occurred in the past 25 years.

Similarly, this work points out the shortcomings of "interest group theories." It suggests that interest group formulations are not so inaccurate as they are incomplete. Aspects of these explanations are, therefore, combined with more neo-Marxian explanations of the political process, which suggest that the state itself has played a significant role in the fruition of political alienation. Accordingly, the role of the state is examined. It is shown how and why the actions of the state have led to more rapid increases in alienation among members of the middle layers than in other classes within American society.

The work also provides an analysis of the role of macroeconomic factors in the determination of political alienation. Data are presented to demonstrate how the economic structure of the United States has changed and how these changes have had detrimental effects on assessments of the political system. It, therefore, links the neo-Marxian aspects of its thesis with the quantitatively oriented literature and shows how a qualitatively better explanation results from a synthesis of these perspectives.

Splitting the Middle also examines the class-based consequences of political alienation. It argues that various factions of the middle layers have developed different short-term interests. They have developed different outlooks, policy preferences, and perceptions of the operation of the state. But even when given the *same* perceptions of the state, different elements of the middle layers have responded quite differently. For example, given the same levels of political distrust and efficacy, members of the new layer (i.e., professionals and managers in the state sector) are more likely than their private sector brethren to engage simultaneously in protest and conventional politics. Similarly, they are far less likely than the traditional working class to drop out of political activity when confronted with political distrust or feelings that the government is not being responsive to their needs and interests.

Splitting the Middle also examines the macro-level consequences of political alienation. It argues that the effects of alienation on the society depend on the political context in which such disaffection occurs. In the late 1960s and early 1970s, high levels of political alienation posed severe challenges to the very operation of the state because alienation was politicized and acted as the basis for mobilizing middle-layer and underdog groups against policies of the state. By the mid to late 1970s, however, high levels of alienation were not as problematic to state managers because progressive groups had demobilized. Nevertheless, the existence of political alienation had the effect of politicizing previously taken-for-granted activities and occurrences. The bases for evaluating the activities of the state were changed qualitatively, and the nature and ground rules for class struggle were altered such that it became virtually impossible for state managers to use pre–1960s methods to solve the problems they faced.

   Finally, *Splitting the Middle* examines the more recent past and suggests what these patterns portend for the post-Reagan years. It suggests that a number of policy choices under the Reagan administration were consistent with the general thesis presented throughout the chapters. It points to the repoliticization of such issues as the budget deficit, tax policy, and social welfare policy as issues that will continue to divide the middle layers and make the range of policy preferences more extreme and divisive.

Why look at, middle layers?

Chapter One

The Middle Layers and Political Alienation

Less than half of the electorate voted in the election that saw George Bush become President. Despite a media blitz that enlisted the endorsements of celebrities and political figures, the turnout in 1988 continued the general downward spiral that began in the mid–1960s. Although some might not view such trends in nonvoting as threatening to democratic outcomes (e.g., Crozier et al. 1975), most people do consider them disturbing. It is no coincidence that these patterns in nonvoting parallel trends in political alienation. Indeed, to the degree that patterns in nonparticipation in the formal electoral process correspond to declines in trust and confidence in elected officials and the political institutions, it could be argued that nonvoting represents a threat to the health of the polity.

Even theorists who see nonvoting as an acceptable form of political expression—especially when it occurs among those "uninformed" members of the electorate who "overload" the system with their "particularistic" demands—become alarmed when nonvoting gives way to more assertive kinds of political participation. When, for example, giving up on the ballot comes to mean taking part in riots, protest marches, or other forms of unconventional political activities, nonvoting becomes *very* problematic. Such modes of political expression, after all, are thought to provide severe threats to democracy.

When it comes to unconventional political involvement, however, most Americans have become accustomed to surges of protest and activism among blacks, the poor, and other groups that do not routinely have their interests served by the operation of the polity. Because these groups often bear the brunt of state policies geared toward promoting "economic growth," most people would not be very astonished to hear that these underdog groups will on many other occasions be locked out of the political process and merely withdraw in defeat. Thus, when mobilization among rather powerless groups takes place in geographically constricted locations, such incidents are now treated as short-term, isolated "crises" that must be "managed."

In the recent past, however, both activism and acquiescence have emerged from a source that might be a bit more surprising—"the middle layers." These professional members of the working class, despite lifestyles that were more affluent than those of others in their class, have become more prone to involvement in protest activities.

These middle layers are two contradictory strata of the working class: the "new layer" and the "professional-managerial class." In many respects they are the embodiment of the class conflicts inherent in capitalist systems. Despite a number of socioeconomic similarities, they have followed different political paths. For example, with the ever-increasing number of recessions and economic downturns in the 1970s, members of the new layer experienced job insecurities, deskilling, and proletarianization of their work. They felt that they were victims of efforts by the government to balance its budget at the same time that it sought to promote corporate gain. They suffered through feelings of betrayal by structures that stripped them of their dignity, autonomy, and vigor. Consequently, this fraction of the middle layers, though they grew up believing in the American way, experienced dramatic declines in their trust and confidence in their governing institutions. They started resorting to strategies of social change, which they previously had regarded as being off limits and out of bounds.

Meanwhile, the professional-managerial class, another portion of the working class that had somewhat higher levels of confidence in the political institutions, became more pessimistic about and unsupportive of America's political institutions. Their faith in America, their government, and the directions of social policy were shaken during the 1960s and early 1970s. They became weary of bearing the burden of the thankless poor. They felt that the price that government representatives asked them to pay for the expanding welfare apparatus was just too high and not worthwhile. They, too, experienced substantial declines in their trust and confidence in government leaders.

There is little doubt that, since the mid–1960s, America's political institutions have experienced dramatic declines in the levels of trust and confidence granted to them (Herring 1987). A number of studies, most of them drawing on data from the National Election Surveys, have verified that political contentment has dropped sharply for more than 25 years (e.g., House and Mason 1975; Lipset and Schneider 1983; J. D. Wright 1976; Herring 1987). These declines have been differentiated by class position. As will be demonstrated throughout this study, they reflect varying levels of disappointment with the policies of the state. In addition, *within* classes there have been wide variations in levels of satisfaction with government policies. For example, policies aimed at spurring economic growth have had several unforeseen effects. They have brought about changes in the composition and living conditions of the working class, and in turn, these changes have led to heterogeneity among workers. Members within the same class have developed qualitatively different short- and medium-run interests. They have also developed different outlooks, policy preferences, and perceptions of the operation of the state. Not only have these class fractions acquired different perceptions, but also—when they have shared the *same* sentiments—they have often responded very differently. For example, when experiencing the same levels of distrust and efficacy, middle-layer workers have been more likely than their traditional working-class counterparts to engage in political dualism (i.e., the simultaneous use of protest and conventional politics).

Levels of political alienation have been rising more rapidly among the middle layers as a whole than among other classes and class fractions. These patterns hold true even once one takes into account a number of sociodemographic factors that tend to offset disaffection. Yet, various segments of these class fractions became very dissimilar from each other in terms of how they reacted to the sources of their political sentiments.

Why did such polarization occur among members of the middle layers? What happened to bring about such divergent patterns among people with ostensibly similar stations in life? How did these factions respond to their varying circumstances? This study will show that from the 1960s through the 1980s, the American state, in efforts to bolster its flagging legitimacy while also trying to stimulate economic growth, engaged in policies that simultaneously squeezed the middle layers by relegating growing proportions of the new layer into economic misery and infuriated those in the new professional-managerial class, who were more able to escape the deleterious effects of the state's fiscal policies.

In addition, industrialization, instead of homogenizing the middle strata, actually divided them. Some workers, especially professional ones in the state sector who earned their living by providing services to people rather than profits to corporations, became divided in their allegiances. They identified with business people and managers in many aspects of their life-styles and outlooks, but with the traditional working class and the poor in their politics. Although some members of the new layer were closely allied with businessmen, they were not closely tied to business interests in civic life because they saw themselves as a self-sufficient working middle class, which was distinct from both the dependent poor and the privileged rich. Thus, in the mid–1960s their image of the government was shaded by movement activities in which they saw the repressive side of the state. They became increasingly negative and cynical, since they saw the government as having a bias against the underprivileged and underdogs of society. Thus, forces that grew out of the early 1960s led to the development of this substantial progressive element in the middle layers that became disenchanted with the price of "economic growth." They saw themselves as having little to gain from a government that promoted corporate interests over the interests of their communities.

While other members of the middle layers were predominantly conservative, these possessors of cultural capital were not. Their increasing expressions of disaffection led to even more social programs. Inasmuch as the movement activity of the 1960s had undermined the authority of state managers, these progressives were able to take advantage of the relative weakness of the state. They were able to challenge the prerogatives of the state and force it into giving them more access to influence the decisions that affected them and those they represented and worked for. As a consequence, the size of this stratum of the middle layers swelled during the war on poverty. The people who tended to fill the positions in those newly expanded programs were more progressive than other segments of the middle layers. Also, it became increasingly clear to them that it was in their interest to seek an even larger welfare state and to pursue other progressive initiatives.

The response of the state was one of oscillation: Initially, it acceded to the demands of those associated with the civil rights movement, the women's movement, the poor people's movements, and other progressive movements seeking economic democracy and social justice; later, it eschewed the ideals of participatory democracy in favor of the demands for material success put forth by corporatist and capitalist interests. The overall effect of such actions by policymakers was to accelerate growing schisms among those in the middle strata and to heighten the levels of political alienation for all groups in the society. This political disaffection, in turn, gave rise to both partisan activism and acquiescence among America's middle layers.

IDENTIFYING THE MIDDLE LAYERS

So far, this discussion has used terms such as "new middle class," "the new layer," "middle strata," "contradictory strata," "middle class," "working middle class," "professional-managerial class," and "middle layers" to refer to those in the class structure who neither fall squarely in the dominant "capitalist class" nor the subordinate traditional "working class," but who fall somewhere between these class locations and have qualities that distinguish them from both. In part, this vagueness is attributable to an acknowledgment that there is no consensus about the nature of the class system in the contemporary United States. Even among those who agree on the number of classes and the characteristics of these classes, there are disagreements about where the lines of demarcation occur and how one can best characterize the members of particular classes or class fractions. Nevertheless, this section will attempt to explain more precisely who is included in the middle layers, as well as related designations.[1]

American scholarship has produced an abundance of meanings and indicators of the concept of class. Those who have attempted to quantify the effects and determinants of class have usually identified class as a subjective condition, as a distinction between levels of education, income, occupational prestige and status, or as a differentiation between manual and nonmanual or blue- and white-collar occupations (e.g., Centers 1949; Hodge and Treiman 1968; Kohn 1977; and Jackman and Jackman 1983).

In contrast, Marxian scholars have defined class as one's relationship to the means of production (e.g., Cottrell 1984). To this traditional conceptualization, neo-Marxians have added the idea of one's position in the social relations in production; that is, one's degree of control over what he or she produces and his or her amount of autonomy in the labor process (e.g., Gouldner 1979; Edwards 1979; Ehrenreich and Ehrenreich 1978). Proponents of this perspective argue that there are hierarchies with both qualitative and quantitative gradations; the former take place between classes, and the latter occur within classes. For reasons that are theoretically central, research based on this model of class requires the maintenance of distinctions between qualitative and quantitative differences.

For the most part, Marxians have rejected the notions and operationalizations of class that non-Marxists have offered on the grounds that they do not adequately capture the crucial dimensions of class. Indeed, Robinson and Kelley (1979) supported this contention with an empirical analysis that concluded that class as conceptualized in the Marxian and neo-Marxian literatures refers to dimensions not tapped by those who use non-Marxist operationalizations of the concept. Fortunately, there have been some recent successes by Marxians in identifying dimensions of class and developing valid indicators that do incorporate the core areas of concern.

Though they concur in naming the capitalist (bourgeoisie) and working (proletariat) classes, these formulations disagree on the number, proportions, and compositions of the classes. In particular, there is continuing debate about whether and how to identify those historically evolving, structural locations that stand between the bourgeoisie and the proletariat and other "class fractions" within these classes. Erik Wright and his associates, for example, refer to positions that are "objectively torn between the antagonistic classes" as "contradictory locations within class relations." Defining classes in terms of common structural positions within the social organization of production, he categorizes these structural positions in terms of three basic criteria: (1) ownership or nonownership of the means of production; (2) purchase or sale of labor power; and (3) control or noncontrol of labor power of workers. His scheme yields four major class categories: (a) *capitalists*, who own the means of production, purchase labor power in order to derive profit from it, and control the labor power of others; (b) *managers*, who do not own the means of production, but do sell their labor power and do control the labor power of others; (c) *workers*, who do not own the means of production, but do sell their labor power and do not control the labor power of others; and (d) the *petite bourgeoisie* who own the means of production, but neither purchase nor sell labor power, and do not control the labor power of others. For this formulation, managers are a "contradictory location," but managers and the petite bourgeoisie, both of which share characteristics with capitalists and workers, are in the middle layers.

In contrast, Alvin Gouldner (1979) argues that besides capitalists and workers, a "new class" of intellectuals, technical experts, and professionals now exists, which derives social power and unity from its possession and control of knowledge, credentials, and "cultural capital." Because these assets are as much "capital as are a factory's bulildings or machines" (p. 25), they too can be the basis for class formation. Moreover, because members of the new class have a distinctive cultural capital, they are united and set apart materially and ideologically from the traditional working class and the old-guard capitalist class.

Similarly, Barbara and John Ehrenreich (1979) suggest that a new "professional-managerial class" (PMC) has come into fruition. For the Ehrenreichs, the PMC includes "those salaried mental workers who do not own the means of production and whose major function in the social division of labor may be described broadly as the reproduction of capitalist culture and capitalist class relations" (p. 12). They stress that the PMC is a heterogeneous class with a wide range of positions. Because of their unique market capacity, however, members of the PMC are generally advantaged compared with members of the working class. Thus, they often have short-run interests that conflict with those of traditional workers. However, this class is also actively and continuously at odds with the capitalist class over control and autonomy in the workplace.

In a similar vein, Nicos Poulantzas (1975) writes about the "new petty bourgeoisie." He claims that this class, consisting of unproductive "mental" labor, cannot be considered part of the working class, and as a whole is in a class that shares some fundamental similarities with the traditional petty bourgeoisie. This nonmanual sector constitutes a distinct class whose members neither own the means of production nor produce surplus value; yet, this class is antagonistic to workers because metal labor dominates manual labor at the ideological level (since capitalists use "unproductive labor" in carrying out the management and supervision of productive workers). In other words, he argues that members of the new petty bourgeoisie cannot occupy positions of ideological domination over the working class and at the same time be members of the working class themselves. In addition, Poulantzas argues, the new petty bourgeoisie are distinguished from the proletariat by "a series of rituals, know-how, and 'cultural elements' " (p. 258), which provide a further basis for ideological differentiation.

C. Wright Mills (1951) places all white-collar workers in the "new middle class" because such people do not produce surplus value, do not own the means of production, and share a distinctive market capacity and work situation in which "they are masters of the commercial, professional, and technical" (p. 65). He goes on to say that white-collar people "keep track; they man the paper routines involved in distributing what is produced. They provide technical and personal services, and they teach others the skills which they themselves practice." (pp. 65–86). In short, Mills distinguishes the new middle class from the working class by the fact that the former consists of unproductive labor. He differentiates the new middle class from the capitalist class on the basis of its nonownership of the means of production.

Finally, more centrist thinkers suggest that there is an "anomalous" quality surrounding this "new class" (e.g., Brint 1984). In particular, while this segment is one of the more privileged in the society, it is not as conservative as one might expect. Indeed, despite their relative affluence, there is evidence to suggest that portions of the so-called new class are actually antiestablishment in their orientations (e.g., Brint 1984).

New class theorists disagree on the defining characteristics and boundaries of the middle. Nevertheless, they make a convincing case that there is a need to recognize and discern the existence of new middle tiers that share neither the objective (immediate) interests nor ideological commitments and outlooks of the capitalist class and the traditional working class. The primary purpose here is not to prove the superiority of one conception of the class structure over others, but rather to point out the existence of such a tier that differs qualitatively from both the bourgeoisie and the proletariat, to demonstrate that contradictory elements within these middle strata have become manifest during periods of heightened political alienation, and to show how and why these increases in cynicism have led to dual tendencies among those in the middle-class fractions. Toward this end, it is necessary to identify who constitutes the middle layers and how they differ from other classes and class fractions.

Generally, the middle layers are noncapitalists who rely on their ability to sell their labor power as a means of making their livelihood. Not only can the middle layers be contrasted with the capitalist class, but also one can differentiate them from the traditional working class and the poor who routinely are unable to sell their labor power at wages sufficient for their viability. As used here, the term "middle layers" is not inconsistent with formulations that point to one's relationship to the means of production and one's social relations in production as the defining criteria of "class."

The middle layers are composed of two class fractions: the professional-managerial class (PMC) and the new layer. Strictly speaking, they can be considered as part of the working class, though as will become clear below, they are substantially different from other workers in many respects.

The Professional-Managerial Class

Consistent with the Ehrenreich's (1979) seminal formulation, the PMC can be identified "as consisting of salaried mental workers who do not own the means of production, and whose major function in the social division of labor may be described broadly as the reproduction of capitalist culture and capitalist class relations" (p. 12). By this definition, the PMC includes people with various occupations, income levels, skills, power, and prestige. According to Noble (1979), the PMC makes up almost one-fourth of the U.S. population (about 50 million people). Contrary to the assertions of the Ehrenreichs, however, the PMC does not constitute a coherent class, in, of, and for itself; rather, they are more accurately viewed as a stratum in the class structure that shares a particular life-style, educational patterns, kinship networks, consumption patterns, ideologies, etc.

The professional-managerial class contributes directly to the maintenance and reproduction of class relations. They are employed in the private sector of the economy, and they are expected to expand profit levels by helping in the expropriation of surplus value from other workers or by producing surplus value themselves. They acquire and transmit their class position through a certification process based upon higher education. Indeed, among the tenets of the ideology of the PMC are beliefs in meritocracy, individualism, professional autonomy, scientific rationality, and the disinterested objectivity of expertise. Such ideological positions allow members of the PMC to see themselves as mediators between capitalists and workers. They do not see themselves as promoting the interests of a ruling class over those of a subdominant classes; rather, they see themselves as speaking for the society in general. Along similar lines, members of the professional-managerial class see themselves neither as a "revolutionary vanguard" seeking social change and equality, nor as "defenders of the status quo." Built into their image of themselves is the idea that they are proficient unbiased mavins who seek efficiency and progress.

Members of the professional-managerial class reap some benefits from the exploitation of traditional workers that takes place under capitalism; yet their labor power, too, is often subject to arrogation by capital, and their skills are vulnerable to degradation, as well. Moreover, much like others in the working class, because this element represents themselves neither in "production politics" nor in "global politics," they are at times denied their dignity, alienated from their labor, and victimized by alienated politics. In short, what Wright (1982) aptly argues about "managers" is generally true of the PMC: They are "locations within the social relations of production that (1) dominate the working class, (2) are dominated by the bourgeoisie, and (3) are exploited by capital, but (4) are exploited to a lesser extent than are [traditional] workers" (p. 335).

The New Layer

Like the professional-managerial class, the new layer consists of those workers who do not own the means of production, but who are unequivocally advantaged in the workplace because they possess sufficient levels of autonomy, expertise, and cultural capital to exercise control over their own labor. In contrast to members of the PMC, workers in the new layer do not routinely extract surplus value from the labor of others. Also, because they are more likely than members of the PMC to work outside the profit-oriented sector, they are less likely to use their skills in the direct production or expropriation of surplus value. Generally, they are professionals in the government and nonprofit sectors, artists, intellectuals, and other semiautonomous employees who, while they must sell their labor power in order to live, do command real control over their own labor power. It is not that these workers are employed in occupations different from the PMC; rather, it is the fact that they procure their livelihoods through means that do not require allegiance to corporations or to the operation of capitalism that is consequential for their politics.

Consistent with Erik Wright's arguments, the new layer is a contradictory location within class relations that can be distinguished not only from the capitalist class, but also from the traditional working class. Despite the new layer's being advantaged when compared with the traditional working class, they are still socially, politically, and econom-ically subordinate under capitalism; despite the fact that they have con-trol over the labor process, members of the new layer are still dominated. Unlike their professional-managerial class counterparts, however, they usually are only indirectly subject to the directives of capital. They are more directly accountable to managers of the state apparatus. They, therefore, are more wary of "big business" than they are of "big gov-ernment." They are more likely than are members of the PMC to ac-knowledge exploitation and inequity, and are, accordingly, more prone to favor political policies that will eradicate such conditions. Finally, unlike the capitalist and the traditional working classes, which are in-herently polarized and antagonistic toward each other, the new layer has some of the relational characteristics of each class and constantly grapples with their own internal contradictions.

DEFINING POLITICAL ALIENATION

For Marx, alienation is an objective condition that exists when social structural forces, especially in the workplace, constrain people and pre-vent them from realizing their human potentials. For him, alienation is most generally the result of overregulation and the imposition of con-straints from external sources. "Alienated man is dehumanized by being conditioned and constrained to see himself, his products, his activities and other men in economic, political, religious and other categories— in terms which deny his and their human possibilities" (Lukes 1967, p. 135).

Neo-Marxians' usage of the term "alienation" closely parallels Marx's use of the term "entausserung" in *Capital*, where he discusses alienation as a condition in which a process of extraction or appropriation of labor power and subsequent reimposition of that power as an alien objectified force takes place. Also, in the *Economic and Philosophical Manuscripts of 1844* Marx identifies characteristics of capitalist production that lead to the estrangement of labor. He discusses several relationships in which the alienation of labor can be seen: (1) in the relationships between laborers and the *products* of their labor; (2) in the relationships between workers and the *act of production* itself; (3) in the relationships between laborers and *their own bodies, external nature, mental lives, and human lives*; and (4) in relationships *among laborers*.

"Alienated politics" proponents, by way of analogy, suggest that po-litical alienation exists when the governing and civic institutions extract power from citizens and subsequently reimpose that power in the form of decisions and policies that have deleterious effects on those from whom the power was originally derived. In other words, political alien-ation is an objective condition that exists when political institutions are not serving the interests of the governed, irrespective of what people *think*. It is the opposite of authentic political representation.

Generally speaking, these neo-Marxian alienated-politics theories, while not focusing on the more humanistic dimensions of alienation, share more commonalities with humanistic and traditional (Marxian) conceptions than they do with their mainstream counterparts. For example, both traditional and neo-Marxian perspectives contend that alienation is relational; that is, they would specify that political alienation is not a characteristic of the individual, but rather it is a description of the relationship between actors and their political structures. Both would also agree that when policymakers do not represent the interests of those who empowered them, an alienating structure exists and the unrepresented citizen is alienated. Also, both views link alienation to the desired performances of policymakers, as alienation exists when the policy outputs do not correspond to the needs of citizens. Finally, both views include the idea that alienation is structurally determined and that its distribution (in terms of its severity) parallels the structure of power in the society.

In contrast, proponents of more mainstream "political disaffection" theories have viewed political alienation as a subjective condition. From this perspective, political alienation is an evaluation of the performance of civic institutions and leaders. It is an opinion. Social scientists working within this framework have tended to shy away from grand theorizing. They have offered theories of the middle range, which for the most part have been empirical in orientation.

A number of political disaffection formulations have been derived from the work of Seeman (1959). Analysts have used modified versions of Seeman's typology to examine such dimensions of political alienation as "political powerlessness," "political meaninglessness," "political normlessness," and "political isolation." Many other terms have become synonymous with political alienation: cynicism, distrust, inefficacy, estrangement, and disaffection. Because these attempts have been, for the most part, based on survey research methodology, they have relied on measures of "felt" disaffection. They have changed the Marxian notion of "objective" alienation into attitude scales, which at times pay little attention to the fundamental sources of alienation. Moreover, they often correlate respondents' attitudes with personal and sociodemographic characteristics without clearly spelling out linkages. Several of their notions of alienation appear only indirectly related to the Marxian counterpart.

With respect to identifying the causes of political alienation, there have been some general tendencies among political disaffection theorists: (1) the attribution of political alienation to "the spirit of the times"; (2) the correlation of sociodemographic characteristics of individuals with political alienation; (3) the linking of political alienation to specific social, political, and economic events and issue attitudes; and (4) the usage of ad hod and post hoc explanations that do not make explicit the theoretical linkages between political alienation and a particular set of findings. These tendencies have not been mutually exclusive of each other; however, because much of the theorizing has been implicit rather than explicit, it is difficult to say what these political disaffection approaches see as the general (underlying) root causes of political alienation.

Social scientists looking at social survey indicators of political alienation have not paid much attention to the formulations and predictions that neo-Marxian (alienated politics) theorists have offered. Likewise, proponents of the neo-Marxian perspectives often have dismissed the methods and findings of those who have attempted to measure and quantify political alienation and related ideas. Only rarely have social scientists from one camp paid much attention to political alienation as conceptualized by the other. It has been more common for the practitioners of the competing approaches to discount and disregard each other.

This disregard is attributable to a combination of epistemological, methodological, and ideological factors: (1) the reluctance of Marxian social scientists to employ "positivist" and "bourgeois" methods to demonstrate or test empirically that which is "dialectical" or that which is true by definition; (2) the unwillingness of non-Marxians to use what they claim to be "nonrigorous" methods; (3) the difficulties involved in trying to operationalize complex, multidimensional Marxian concepts; (4) the unsuitable nature of much existing data for testing Marxian formulations; and (5) the lack of dialogue between the Marxian and non-Marxian literatures.

In short, what Wright and Perrone (1977) pointed out more than a decade ago continues to be true today: "Marxists have been suspicious of quantitative, multivariate approaches to the study of social reality, and the practitioners of multivariate statistics generally have viewed the Marxist perspective as offering little of interest for empirical research" (p. 32). Thus, gaps between these two literatures exist and differences between them persist. But as will be pointed out below, maybe it is now both feasible and desirable to bridge some of these gaps.

POLITICAL ALIENATION AND THE MIDDLE LAYERS: BRIDGING SOME GAPS

Social researchers using survey indicators of political alienation have reported a trend toward higher levels of cynicism, distrust, inefficacy, estrangement, and disaffection. These social scientists have pointed out that the levels and incidence of political alienation are not uniform across the American populace, but rather they indicate that there are identifiable social groups in which the higher levels and rates of political alienation are concentrated. In general, these researchers have found that it is people with memberships in groups with low structural locations who have the higher levels and rates of political alienation: nonwhites, women, the poor, the uneducated, the old, etc. Political alienation is, however, also increasing within most other segments of the American population, including the middle orders.

Meanwhile, neo-Marxian alienated politics theorists have argued that the political institutions of the United States are moving toward a "legitimacy crisis." According to these theorists, during this legitimacy crisis, the role of the state and its constituent parts will be called into question by groups mobilized to effect changes in the operation and results of liberal democracy. Generally, they argue that the capitalist state has become increasingly involved in supporting the process of capital accumulation for corporations and the capitalist class. As this has proceeded, citizens—especially those most adversely affected by such state involvement—have ceased to support the actions and policies of the government, elected officials, and the political institutions. The bulk of the citizenry, then, has become more alienated from the political institutions of the state, and the state itself has become the target of discontent and the object of struggle.

Neo-Marxian theorists have predicted a rise in political alienation and a decline in the state's legitimacy; survey researchers monitoring indicators of political alienation have detected decreases in support for the political institutions of the United States. What follows is an attempt to delineate, test, and correct the various explanations of increasingly negative assessments of the American state. In pursuing these goals, this work discusses contributions and limitations of mainstream "political disaffection" explanations and neo-Marxian "alienated politics" formulations. More importantly, it offers an alternative, more comprehensive explanation that more closely fits the patterns of change in assessments of America's political institutions.

It argues that challenges to the legitimacy of the American state will come not from the poor and other groups lacking access to the state apparatus, but rather from those in the middle layers. Although those in the middle components traditionally have benefited from state activity, increasingly they are threatened with losing their position because economic stagnation and contraction undermine the bases of their relative privilege. The central thesis here is that the underlying driving force behind increases in political alienation and subsequent activism and acquiescence is state policies, that have relegated greater proportions of the middle strata to conditions of economic misery. Changes in the

levels of economic misery among the middle layers, in turn, have triggered changes in their perceptions of the state's effectiveness in dealing
with their problems and responding to their needs.

Of course, several other factors have effects on political alienation and
assessments of state legitimacy. For example, previous research has suggested that several sociodemographic variables affect levels of political
alienation. The chapters to follow will demonstrate that many of these
effects can be "explained" by macro-levels variables that generally reflect
state policies. Nevertheless, many of the patterns of change in political
alienation can be attributed to elements consistent with variants of political disaffection explanations that emphasize political structures and
interest groups. In fact, the central argument will incorporate group-
based formulations to explain why the middle orders experienced dramatic increases in political alienation. Also, it will point to ideological
predispositions consistent with political disaffection perspectives to account for the conditions under which undirected cynicism will be transformed into politicized disaffection, which mobilizes portions of the
middle fragments and leads them to call into question the actions of the
state. In addition, it will suggest that highly visible social movement
activity by groups mobilized to effect change acted as catalyzing elements. The existence of such movement activity affected not only the
willingness of people to engage in unconventional political activity, but
also their perceptions of how well the state was managing the affairs of
the people. In short, the present explication will attempt to incorporate
factors from competing mainstream and critical literatures. It will syn-
thesize them into a more fruitful and empirically accurate explanation
of why growing proportions of Americans have come to believe that
their government, political leaders, policymakers, and political institutions are not responsive to their problems, needs, and interests.

In the chapters that follow, however, this study will show how far
off the mark existing explanations are in terms of predicting patterns of
change in political alienation and responses to those changes. It will
become more clear that the alternative explanation, while not perfect,
makes substantial and qualitative improvements over existing theories.

NOTE

1. One of the major drawbacks of secondary analysis is that it does not always
allow analysts to operationalize variables and concepts optimally. Such was the
case with the primary source of data used in this study: the 1964–80 American
National Election Surveys. Optimal designation of the two middle-layer strata
would have led to a division based on whether respondents had professional
or managerial employment in the state sector, irrespective of their specific occupations. However, because these surveys did not ask respondents whether
they worked for the government, professional or supervisory occupations in the
following industries were designated as the sources of new-layer membership:

public administration, nonprofit membership organizations, residential welfare facilities, welfare services, religious organizations, museums, art galleries, zoos, educational services, hospitals, convalescent institutions, health services, colleges and universities, libraries, and utilities and sanitary services. For other sources of data that did ask respondents whether they worked for the government (such as the General Social Surveys), professional and managerial workers were classified as members of the new layer if they reported that they worked for the government.

That's all he says!

Chapter Two

Splitting the Middle

In every society, there exist some beliefs that are so all-pervasive that they influence the lives and behaviors of virtually everyone. These views become so ingrained that they, at times, take on a "natural-order-of-things," taken-for-granted character. Under certain conditions, however, these hegemonic ideologies can be eradicated, at least among sub-populations whose interests are not well-served by such tenets.

In the United States, beliefs in personal property, individualism, and freedom of choice are among the core ideas that go relatively unchallenged. Prior to the 1960s and 1970s a number of other ideas were also established doctrines of the American creed: segregation of the races, disenfranchisement of blacks, lower pay and status for women, obedience to the dictates of the state, and the notion that corporate actors could make production and investment decisions without regard to the consequences such decisions would have on their communities.

During the relatively unique circumstances of the 1960s and 1970s, however, a number of happenings converged to call into question the validity of these positions. The civil rights movement, the women's movement, and the Vietnam War, in conjunction with changes in the relative power of the working class (due to alterations in labor market and industrial structures), eroded the state's ability to claim neutrality in conflicts. No longer could the state officially sanction the denial of basic civil rights to blacks without being perceived as a racist state. No longer could it condone legal discrimination against women without being seen as a patriarchal state. No longer could it compel its citizens to fight and die in unjust wars without being viewed as an authoritarian state. And no longer could it openly champion the interests of the capitalist class in the name of the society at large without being regarded as a capitalist state.

In the course of pursuing their goals, the social movements of the 1960s and 1970s exposed millions of members of the middle layers to the biases of the state. At the same time, the policies of the state were plunging ever-growing proportions of the middle layers into economic despondency. Yet because not all of the sympathies of the middle layers were aligned with the same causes, and because the adverse consequences of the state's policies were not universally felt by all members of the middle layers, the actions of these movements and the subsequent reactions of the state had the overall effect of splitting the middle.

On the one hand, a large portion of the middle layers, particularly those who were rapidly beginning to identify with major corporations and business interests, saw progressive elements of the 1960s and 1970s as perversions of American values and as attacks on them and their lifestyles. These members of the middle layers had grown up and become more successful than their parents by steadfastly embracing patriotism, conformity, self-discipline, and material acquisition. When they saw blacks, hippies, militants, and at times even their own sons and daughters behaving in undisciplined ways, destroying and burning the flag, or engaging in other profane acts, they blamed government leaders. When blacks started moving into their neighborhoods, and black children were being bussed into their schools, they felt that the political institutions and leaders were at fault. When antidiscrimination and affirmative action policies started changing the gender composition of the workforce and the complexion of the people on their jobs, they knew the politicians were no longer representing their interests. And when their tax bills started rising to pay for government programs that did not benefit them, but rather benefited those very people who were assailing and trampling their values and aspirations, they became irate. Their levels of political alienation shot up, largely because of what they saw as the inaction of those who were supposedly representing them.

On the other hand, other factions of the middle layers who were joining forces with those seeking social changes had already learned not to trust the system to reform itself. They had learned that things would improve only when they became involved at the grass-roots level. For them, the cost of counting on corporations or the government to right wrongs was just too high. They were not willing to give up the right to make basic decisions, nor were they willing to defer their opinions to those of so-called experts. Transforming society was not to be a spectator sport for them. Though their levels of political distrust were already high, those levels grew precipitously through the 1970s because the economic downturns of this period led them to become concerned about their personal economic security.

Clearly, the events of the 1960s and 1970s did not affect members of the society in the same fashion. Nor did these occurrences have the same effects on those in the middle layers. Indeed, as the expansion of direct democratic participation (in the form of social movement activity and other kinds of collective action) weakened the authority of the state, the middle layers became polarized, as they were not uniform in their levels of class consciousness and their support for the different causes of the era. Even the shrinking economy of the period led to greater polarization of the middle layers, as people were differentially affected and therefore had substantially different views on the appropriateness of the steps taken by the state.

IDEOLOGICAL POLARIZATION, CONSCIOUSNESS, HEGEMONY, AND POLITICAL ACTION

Although the movements of the 1960s had not lived up to their rhetoric, they had started a process of polarization that resulted in a new understanding of class dynamics in the United States. Though venerated in the name of Marxism by some on the left, simple-minded definitions of class based on unidimensional notions of exploitation no longer applied to an America with more than a dialectical struggle between rich and poor. There was no solid, homogeneous working class. The fundamental struggle between capital and labor remained, but also there existed a matrix of class struggle in which affluent and poverty-stricken workers pursued qualitatively different interests. Workers were divided not only by such things as income, but also by such characteristics as race, occupation, wealth, workplace autonomy, and professional status. At times, these attributes acted to pit worker against worker, and thus acted as bases for polarization.

These differences showed up as differences in patterns of change in political alienations, as the positions on key issues of policy became more polarized and ideologically structured. People tended to hold more extreme but consistent attitudes on a number of issues. This pattern of polarization and ideological consistency had its roots in two factors. First, those who were most active in political activities were also most likely to have consistent and systematic views on controversial issues. And because the 1960s were filled with social movement activities and other modes of political activism, they were followed by extreme polarization of political opinion. This increase in polarization, in turn, often led to higher levels of group consciousness that triggered even more participation.

Second, polarization was undoubtedly due to the nature of the controversies that became central to the political agenda of the 1960s. The three major clusters of issues that came to the fore were social issues (e.g., "Great Society programs," civil liberties, and the role of women), racial issues (e.g., busing, voting rights, and equal employment and opportunity), and military issues (e.g., Vietnam, the draft, and military spending).

Divisions over these issues, in addition to concerns about macroeconomic policies, led to major increases in political alienation among various factions of the middle layers. Increasingly, substantial portions of the American public took more extreme positions on these controversies. Often, in attempting not to anger either of the opposing camps, political leaders acted with ambivalence and took the middle road. Instead of appeasing, the politics of compromise and vacillation alienated more and more people who increasingly took extreme positions on the issues.

Political alienation spread well beyond the poor and the traditional working class into the new layer and the PMC—economic and social strata where deep disaffection had seldom been experienced. From the perspective of less progressive elements of the PMC, the system had not only denied them a meaningful voice, but also it had victimized them by demanding that they pay steadily increasing taxes to support a war they did not favor or to provide welfare payments for "lazy nogoods" whom they did not even like. Moreover, this class fraction often felt that they were being singled out as the only group for whom the rules applied: The rich, who made the rules to begin with, could always buy their way out of trouble; the poor, when they wanted something, looted, stole, or murdered to get it. As upstanding citizens who were not immune to the laws of the land, members of the PMC were required to obey the unequally enforced rules, regulations, and laws.

But in the milieu of dissent and upheaval, when the opportunity presented itself in the form of an extraordinary candidate or an urgent issue, portions of the new layer took action. Increasingly, they came to accept, approve of, and participate in strikes, protest marches, and other activities to make their voices heard. Thus, protest politics became an acceptable method of influencing outcomes for them. Because these tactics were often useful in bringing about change in the conditions that this layer wanted changed, strikes and marches by teachers, nurses, government workers, and other professionals became virtually commonplace.

But not all portions of the middle layers engaged in protest activities. In the late 1960s and early 1970s strikes as a protest strategy became increasingly ineffective, as the state began restoring the power of capitalists and corporations by utilizing a monetarist strategy of making jobs scarce. With the economic contractions and recessions that occurred during this period, work stoppages often coincided with corporate desires to slow down production. Thus, higher rates of unemployment helped maintain the position of capital over labor, and very high unemployment rates over long periods helped reverse the ability of the working class to make greater demands on their employers. Consequently, members of the working class who were in capital-dependent jobs were not as prone to join in on antigovernment or anticapital activities during those days of job insecurities.

Members of the free professions, for example, writers, professors, lawyers, and students who were in training to become professionals, were in better positions to take the initiative and most active roles in opposition and protest activities. They were more capable of devoting their time to change efforts. They were more likely to possess organizational skills and economic resources. They had access to legal defense when required. They could not be easily muzzled or silenced, as they often also had relatives and friends to fall back on for assistance when threatened with being prosecuted or punished in some fashion. And they were not as threatened with losing their jobs.

In contrast, lower and middle managers, members of the traditional working class, and other lower-ranking white-collar employees were in far more vulnerable positions. In most cases, they were extremely dependent on the authorities to make their living. They did not have much in the way of free time to devote to causes, even when they did sympathize with the efforts. They were more limited in terms of their material resources. By and large, they were not as likely to possess the organizational skills nor access to powerful others who could bail them out of threatening situations. In short, they had much higher costs associated with their participation in protest activities.

Nevertheless, a number of members of the traditional working class and others who were unshielded did politicize their alienation. At the same time, a number of members of the new layer who were less politically and economically assailable did not join in efforts to try to change the system. Undoubtedly, class "consciousness" played a part in how these members of the middle layers apprehended the requirement for action on their part.

Consciousness—awareness of sharing a similar position in the social structure with others who are willing to join together to oppose aspects of the sociopolitical system that operate against their collective interests—involves several discernible aspects: (1) an examination of how stratification comes about; (2) an interpretation of why stratification operates the way it does; (3) a perception of one's own location in the stratification system; (4) an identification and feeling of solidarity with others similarly situated in the stratification system; (5) a willingness to join in efforts to protect the interests common to one's group; and (6) an evaluation of the workings of the stratification system.

The relevant group consciousness was "underdog group" consciousness; namely that which corresponded to subordinated groups in American society. This consciousness played a role in how members of the middle layers felt toward the government, public officials, and the political process. Because of the capitalist class-biased nature of the American state, a greater percentage of those with underdog group consciousness were alienated from the government and public officials than were those without such apperceptions. Such consciousness translated into group-based action to the degree that it was premised on awareness and identification with the interests of the working class or other underdog groups, rejection of other class interests as illegitimate, beliefs that different class interests conflicted with each other, and willingness to rely on political means to realize working-class interests to the negation of other class interests. On highly publicized, controversial issues, members of the working class knew what their immediate (short-run) interests were, and they favored actions by the state that would have resolved these issues in accordance with their class interests. Class consciousness played a major role in determining policy preferences with respect to these class-based issues.

On a number of issues, however, class interests were not clear cut, and underdog group consciousness played only a negligible part in mobilizing members of the working class. Indeed, a large number of working-class people often subscribed to views formulated by the capitalist class and their employees. Moreover, it is clear that most workers did not usually have "revolutionary" outlooks, but rather were products of capitalist state hegemony.

Could capitalist state hegemony be eradicated among members of the middle layers? Some social theorists would respond with an axiomatic no. They would argue that if an ideology is hegemonic, unchallenged, and noncontroversial, it is by definition unchangeable. The validity of this position is most doubtful. As Edelman (1971, p. 47) points out, "only mass cognitions that are noncontroversial are easily changed." He explains this paradox:

In the case of a consensually held cognition stemming from a monopolistic source of information, . . . [b]ecause the belief is not challenged, there is no need to justify or rationalize it. It is held because the only available cues disseminate it and because the people, similarly cued, reinforce it. By the same token it is readily changed when other source[s] of cues issue different signals (Edelman 1971, pp. 47–48).

If, then, it was possible to change such widely held beliefs, what were to be the mechanisms that would foster such changes? An easy answer to this question would be something to the effect of "consciousness raising." But exactly what such a response means is not all together clear. Edelman suggests a role for the state itself in consciousness raising through its role in policy formation and implementation. He states that "government affects behavior chiefly by shaping the cognitions of large numbers of people in ambiguous situations." It helps create their beliefs about what is proper; their perceptions of what is fact; and their expectations of what is to come" (p. 7). While his points are well-taken, they are not altogether satisfactory for explaining how a consensus-based belief could be replaced, especially because the state had little incentive to change anything that was "consensually based" without a push from some source.

Because "the content of an individual's conceptions of the history and the future of his or her collectivity comes to depend on the processes by which public events get constructed as resources for discourse in public matters" (Molotch 1974, pp. 102–3), some people would point to the mass media as a source of consciousness raising that served to undermine capitalist state hegemony. However, to the degree that the middle layers did not have control of or even significant access to the media, it was virtually impossible that they had any serious impact on the general population or any subpopulation through the media. Taken by itself, then, this approach is also found to be lacking.

A final approach to eliminating capitalist state hegemony involves primary group and grass-roots activism and participation. These approaches are based on the notion the sources of counterlegitimacy generated in movement-related primary groups lays the basis for taking on new roles, beliefs, and outlooks. Bennett (1975, p. 152), for example, argues that:

(1) grassroots activism is likely to immerse the individual in direct conflict over political issues and social values. Cognitive changes resulting from these experiences should influence, to the greatest possible extent, the citizen's ability to think about the issues and values that are directly related to public policy . . . (2) grassroots activism represents a means of changing mass political consciousness that does not presume a systematic program of social and cultural reform . . . (3) grassroots activities are modes of experience over which each individual participant has a high degree of control . . . and (4) grassroots activities are modes of experience that permit comparatively easy involvement, given few facilitating conditions.

The proponents of this approach believe that primary group and grass-roots activism will be effective in raising consciousness in that this approach posits, as one of its cornerstone assumptions, that values, atti-

tudes, and outlooks are learned, supported, and reinforced in primary
groups and other intimate, face-to-face interactions. While this approach
to consciousness raising is more appealing than the alternatives presented here, it too is incomplete unless it can somehow make links
between the individual, the primary and grassroots groups, and the
larger political structure.

While none of the approaches presented here are sufficient in and of
themselves to account for challenges to the capitalist state, they do suggest that such a task was not impossible. In particular, explanations that
point to grass-roots activism and participation, especially when coupled
with the polarizing effects of policy blunders, go a long way toward
explaining how and why the capitalist state lost a great deal of its capacity
to continue portraying itself as a legitimate representative of noncapitalists.

RAISING CONSCIOUSNESS AND TEARING DOWN HEGEMONY

When Lyndon Baines Johnson first took the oath of office in 1963, no
one could have guessed what was in store for America. Johnson had
successfully managed the "succession crisis," and in his first full term
as president he found himself with a liberal majority. Surely there would
be no real limits to what he could accomplish. Such thinking was rooted
in the vision of a "Great Society" agenda that Johnson had laid out.
However, this vision occurred *before* the riots at Watts occurred, *before*
Vietnam was something more than a small, distant conflict, and *before*
other controversies tore the nation apart.

The social movements of the 1960s, for example, ushered in a new
era in American politics. These movements succeeded in educating a
new coalition of dissidents and activists by unveiling to a growing number of people the various faces of the political system. In the final analysis, however, these movements were not the *cause* of the "crisis of
confidence" that hounded the political institutions of the state; rather,
they acted as facilitators by providing a context in which antigovernment
sentiments were made acceptable and by providing a vehicle to express
such sentiments. These movements, by identifying and distilling key
issues and mapping out strategies to confront them, helped people to
better understand the nature of their society and their government.

Under the capable leadership of the Reverend Dr. Martin Luther King,
Jr., and others, the civil rights movement did many things that ran
against the American grain. It challenged America to abandon its racial
double standard. It called for the disobedience of authority, laws, and
social norms that were morally bankrupt. It called on people to love
those who hated them. It required men and women to fight injustice

nonviolently. In addition, it relied on tactics that fell outside of the formal political process to change the political system. Locations such as Montgomery (where blacks boycotted the bus system) and Greensboro (where they sat-in at whites-only lunch counters) captured the public's imagination. They provided models for vast changes in race relations throughout the country. And in 1963, the March on Washington for Jobs and Freedom provided the vehicle for many sympathizers and allies to endorse the cause. These nonviolent activities communicated a false sense of where the civil rights movement was heading, however. Because these actions suggested that nonviolence was growing in popularity, they tranquilized those who were to be moved to action rather than arousing them.

By 1964, a more angry side of the civil rights movement began making itself known. For example, in February of that year nearly half a million black students boycotted the New York public schools for being segregated. Ghetto residents of that city also engaged in rent strikes. Furthermore, the Congress of Racial Equality (CORE) promoted efforts to block traffic on the city's bridges. The movement had gradually shifted from its first phase in the South, where it was especially concerned with issues such as the right to sit at the front of a bus or the right to be served in a restaurant. It increasingly became involved with more central issues concerning the distribution of economic resources. Its class dimensions became more evident.

In 1965, rioting erupted in Watts, a black section of Los Angeles, California. After five days and nights of burning, 34 people were dead, 4,000 more had been arrested, and millions of dollars in property had been reduced to ashes. While the riot's official origins remain unclear, it is clear that Watts residents suffered from police brutality, economic neglect, and other problems. It was only after the rioting and burnings that Watts residents received antipoverty money. In subsequent years, other locales such as Newark, New Jersey, and Detroit, Michigan experienced similar riots for similar reasons. In the long run, these actions had deleterious effects on the public mood. While they enhanced the political efficacy of ghetto residents and provided funds to ameliorate some of the problems in these communities, these riots tended to increase white backlash. Police departments everywhere equipped themselves with heavy combat weapons. Private citizens armed themselves in growing numbers. And conservative politicians were swept into office on "law-and-order" platforms.

Blacks rioted because whites were not doing enough; however, the riots usually made whites even less willing to do anything. Some conscience money drifted into riot areas. But it was not nearly enough to make up for the homes that were destroyed, the stores and shops that were lost, and the jobs that were to leave forever. The riots were also

Typical of his style: undocumented editorials - no data so far + no detailed theory.

used as an excuse to exterminate radical black groups such as the Black Panthers. Nevertheless, despite the fact that the objective conditions of blacks in riot areas often worsened, their levels of political efficacy frequently increased.

While riots led to white backlash, such movement activities did not really do much to harm the relations between blacks and white progressives. Indeed, members of such progressive groups as the Students for a Democratic Society (SDS) viewed the riots as "revolutionary consciousness-raising experiences" for people making history. The poor and such progressive elements formed mutually reinforcing alliances that pushed for expansion of the welfare state. Together, they pressed the government to recognize the rights of the needy to public assistance. They persuaded relief agencies to be more generous in their benefits. They helped bring about more widespread dissemination of information about welfare rights and benefits. And they helped bring about an expansion of the war on poverty. These triumphs were won through the use of grass-roots activities.

The tactics employed by the movements—demonstrations, sit-ins, pickets, teach-ins, and meetings—provided a mechanism of bringing the issues of protest to ordinary people. Most people did not want to participate in making *all* the decisions that affected them. They did, however, want better policies and state management to improve the quality of their lives. They did want the system to be more responsive to their needs. They did want it to work as well for them as they felt they worked for it. They did want such things as better schools, more comprehensive health care, cleaner air, and greater equality of access. Activists, through the use of their demonstrations, showed not only that the issues were moral ones, but also that direct, grass-roots participation could make a difference. They illustrated that direct action was one way of prodding the state into action or of halting its actions.

But direct action was also a way of unmasking the face of repression that radicals and progressives had claimed the state usually concealed. Agents of the state showed themselves to be not only callous, but also brutal in such locales as Birmingham, Alabama; Kent State, Ohio; Detroit, Michigan; and Berkeley, California. Faith in the system eroded not only among those who were immediately involved, but also among those onlookers who supported their causes and among those who did not believe their government was capable of such brute force against their fellow Americans. For the first time for millions of Americans in the middle layers, civil rights became a real issue that was not too remote from their relative affluence nor too removed from their suburban communities. The growing struggles on university campuses took on the air of being something more significant than college pranks. In addition, Vietnam became an urgent issue, as it affected the sons of the middle layers almost as much as it did blacks and the poor. Protest concerning these issues, especially when greeted with harsh treatment, raised questions about the social (moral), political, and economic priorities of the state. At the same time, attempts by the state to suppress the message of activists proved to them that they were compelling enough to be thought of as real threats to the status quo.

For progressives, the growing sense that the state itself was part of the opposition did little to increase their levels of political trust. The idea that they could act as a threat to their opposition, however, did lead to higher levels of political efficacy and greater demands among them and others who began to sympathize with their views. They pressed for a greater degree of access and inclusion in the process. They pushed for a redistribution of government spending away from the military toward social programs. And ultimately, they played a large role in the expansion of governmental activity and the subsequent establishment of a milieu of political distrust and dissent.

Progressives' attacks on the state also played a significant role in the development of what Samuel Huntington (1975) refers to as "the welfare shift." During the 1960s and 1970s, there were massive increases in government spending for education, social security, public welfare, and other social welfare and entitlement programs. As will be argued later, these increases in spending occurred as the state found itself in greater need of fulfilling its legitimacy function, and they were closely linked to trends in public opinion. Prior to the activities of progressive activists, levels of support for nondefense government programs had been substantially lower than those for defense spending (Huntington 1961). But public opinion on these issues changed dramatically during the 1960s. For example, in 1960 only 18 percent of the public felt that the United States was spending too much on defense, and 21 percent believed that too little was being spent. By 1969, however, 52 percent of the people believed that the United States was spending too much on defense, and only 8 percent felt that the country needed to spend more for defense. At the same time, the weight of public opinion swung in favor of increased spending for virtually all domestic social programs (Watts and Free 1974).

Because state managers attempted to keep pace with progressives' demands for an expanded welfare state, the number and range of programs grew, and the fiscal gaps associated with them took on new proportions. In 1959, the deficit was $17 billion. By 1971, it was $27 billion, and by 1986 it was $226 billion. With the increased demand and support for social programs, calls for ever-larger tax cuts, and no real reductions in military spending, larger and larger deficits seemed inescapable.

These programs and the deficits they spawned, however, represented not only fiscal problems for the state, but also political ones. Although a number of people, including government employees, benefited from the state's new found generosity, others in the society whose interests clearly ran counter to such policies felt that they received few benefits from the government in return for their higher taxes. Because the political basis for the welfare shift was the expansion of direct democratic participation and the heightened dedication to democratic and egalitarian ideals that existed among those influenced by the movements of the 1960s, the conditions that catalyzed large-scale, wide-ranging, social programs vanished after the levels of political activism declined. Nevertheless, once many of these programs were established, it was difficult for state managers to try to dismantle them. At the same time, not dismantling them had high political costs, as those who derived no benefits from such policies saw the government as getting too powerful and bloated.

In addition to providing challenges to state managers by providing a basis for polarization over policies, the direct democratic participation of the 1960s and 1970s also served to undermine existing systems of authority. This questioning of authority manifested itself in politics as well as other realms. No longer did people in the street feel the obligation to defer to those whom they had previously thought of as being superior to themselves in rank, expertise, or otherwise. Each group asserted its prerogative to participate fully in those decisions that would have a direct or indirect impact on its members. Authority based on wealth, expertise, or other criteria that ran counter to the egalitarian and democratic principles of the times was readily assailed. On college campuses, students demanded their right to participate in the decision-making process on all issues of importance to them. In bureaucracies, subordinates were less hesitant to criticize or oppose the aims of their organizational superiors. In government, power based on wealth was exposed and challenged through reforms in the system.

Authority based on electoral success was, for the most part, still considered legitimate and consistent with democratic principles. But even in the formal political process, the decrease in obedience to authority manifested itself. There were dramatic declines in confidence and trust in political leaders and institutions, as well as a reduction in the power and effectiveness of the political institutions. Among progressives, the actions of their representatives became viewed as legitimate only to the degree that they promoted egalitarian and participatory goals. These liberal and radical elements (mostly) from the new layer of the working class started displaying more concern for the fairness and content of laws than for the procedures that were used to bring them about. Thus, even the formal electoral process, though not inconsistent with parti-

so far, and soup material, and more on politics than on class

cipatory democracy, was also called into question when it yielded results that were not in keeping with the ideals of social justice and equal rights.

Many of the ideological differences among members of the middle layers that were created during the 1960s and 1970s carried over to the 1980s. Differences in values, priorities, and orientations continued to show up as different policy preferences among those in the middle layers. Despite similarities in such areas as income, educational attainment, and occupational prestige, members of the new layer and the professional-managerial class became very dissimilar politically.

SOCIAL AND DEMOGRAPHIC PROFILES OF THE CLASS LAYERS: THE BASES FOR POLARIZATION

Throughout this study, comparisons between the classes and among the class layers will be presented. For the most part, these differences will be discussed as if social life were *ceteris paribus*. Because the primary area of concern is that of class dynamics, other relevant factors will usually be held constant statistically so that the effects of class position per se can be ascertained. That is, the focus will be on *net* differences that occur across classes and class layers. The analysis will, for example, present relationships between class position and political alienation that hold true once income, gender, and racial differences, to name a few, are taken into consideration.

sel Bourd: you can control away part of the phenomenon.

As reasonable people know, however, all other relevant social facts are hardly ever equal. For that reason, most of net differences between classes and among class layers presented are substantially smaller than what would be reported were sociodemographic differences not taken into account, that is, if only *gross* differences were presented. To provide some idea of the magnitude of the differences that occur across class levels, the remainder of this chapter provides a sociodemographic and political profile of the various class fractions.

note # is an explanatory variable at times above

Table 1 presents several characteristics of the different class fractions. These class traits are presented as percentages and as means. They provide basic descriptions of some of the kinds of similarities and dissimilarities that occur by class location. For example, this table shows, not surprisingly, that the poor rank lowest on such dimensions as educational attainment, income, and occupational prestige. In addition, they tend to be older than members of other class fractions, and they are more likely than members of other class fractions to be black and female.

Table 1 shows that members of the new layer have the highest average levels of educational attainment (14.5 years). They are followed by the PMC with 13.5 years and capitalists with 13.4 years. Members of the

Table 1
Selected Sociodemographic Characteristics of the Class Layers

Sociodemographic Characteristics

Class Layer	Mean Education	Mean Income	Mean Occup. Prestige	Mean Age	%Minority	%Female
Capitalist	13.4	$26928	45.0	46.4	6.0	41.4
PMC	13.5	$26966	47.9	39.8	6.1	52.2
New Layer	14.5	$26808	54.4	47.3	13.8	49.6
Working	12.2	$23037	35.9	43.1	14.4	55.4
Poor	10.3	$6784	30.8	54.7	21.0	65.5

Source: 1985 General Social Survey, National Opinion Research Center.

traditional working class average 12.2 years of schooling. In addition, the poor achieve 10.3 years in school on average.

Table 1 also shows mean income levels by class location. It shows that members of the capitalist class, the PMC, and the new layer have virtually the same levels of income. Members of these class layers average just under $27,000 per year. In contrast, traditional workers average just over $24,000, and the poor receive less than $7,000.

On average, members of the new layer have the highest occupational prestige. Their mean occupational prestige score is 54.4. The PMC attain a mean occupational prestige score of 47.9. Capitalists, traditional workers, and the poor average 45.0, 35.9, and 30.8, respectively.

In terms of age, Table 1 indicates that members of the PMC tend to be younger than people from other class fractions. Their average age is slightly less than 40 years. Members of the traditional working class average 43.1 years, and capitalists average 46.4 years. Members of the new layer have a mean age of 47.3 years, and the poor average 54.7 years.

The racial composition of the class fractions is also presented in Table 1. Blacks and other racial minorities make up roughly 6 percent of the capitalist class and the PMC. The proportions of both the new layer and the traditional working class are more than twice as much, as 13.8 percent and 14.4 percent of these class fractions are either black or from some other racial minority group. In addition, more than 20 percent of the poor are blacks and other racial minorities.

The gender composition of the class fractions is also presented in Table 1. This table shows that about two out of five members of the capitalist class (41.4%) are women. In contrast, nearly two out of three of the poor (65.5%) are women. Slightly less than half of the members of the new

Table 2
Political Views and Orientations of the Class Layers

Political Views and Orientations

Class Layer	%Democrat	%Liberal	%Voting for Reagan in 80	%Voting for Reagan in 84
Capitalist	30.3	24.9	51.6	68.5
PMC	30.1	22.2	56.3	71.6
New Layer	47.1	31.7	38.9	46.2
Working	48.1	26.2	46.7	57.3
Poor	47.4	27.7	37.5	48.4

Source: 1985 General Social Survey, National Opinion Research Center.

here, "new" = prof + managers in gov't

layer (49.6%) are women, and slightly more than half of the PMC (52.2%) and the traditional working class (55.4%) are women.

The results in Table 1 suggest that, with the possible exception of their racial compositions, there are not great demographic differences between the new layer and the PMC. Nor are there dramatic differences between these fractions of the working class and members of the capitalist class. Demographically, the new layer has more in common with the PMC and capitalists than it does with the traditional working class and the poor. However, this is not the case when it comes to political views and orientations.

Table 2 presents the distribution of political views by class location. This table shows that less than one-third of the PMC (30.1%) and the capitalist class (30.3%) identify themselves as Democrats. In contrast, nearly half of the new layer (47.1%), the traditional working class (48.1%), and the poor (47.4%) think of themselves as Democrats.

Table 2 also indicates that members of the new layer are the class fraction most likely to identify themselves as liberal. Nearly one-third of the new layer (30.7%) say that they are liberal. Members of the PMC are the least likely to think of themselves as liberal, as about one-fifth (22.2%) of them claim such ideological predispositions. Other class fractions fall between these ranges, as 24.9 percent of capitalists, 26.2 percent of the traditional working class, and 27.7 percent of the poor are self-identified liberals.

This table reports similar patterns with respect to who voted for Ronald Reagan. In 1980, less than two out of five new-layer voters (38.9%) voted for Reagan. This finding is in contrast to 56.3 percent of PMC voters. In 1984, a smaller percentage of the new layer than any other class fraction cast votes for Reagan, as 46.2 percent voted for him. In contrast, the PMC provided the largest margin of support for the Reagan candidacy, with more than 70 percent of this stratum voting for him. Other class fractions again fell between these extremes, as 68.5 percent of capitalist voters, 57.3 percent of traditional working-class voters, and 48.4 percent of poor voters cast ballots in support of Reagan.

By the mid–1980s, the PMC and the new layer also differed substantially in terms of what the nation's priorities should be. For example, data from the 1985 General Social Survey show that, while the new layer was the class fraction most likely to oppose cuts in government spending, the PMC was the fraction most likely to favor such cuts. A majority of the new layer believed that too much was being spent on the military; a majority of the PMC did not. A significantly larger proportion of the new layer than the PMC favored government support for declining industries to protect jobs. While most of the PMC felt that business taxes were too high or about right (57.7%), an overwhelming majority of the new layer (60.0%) felt that business taxes were, in fact, too low. And while a majority of the new layer favored policies aimed at keeping unemployment down (56.9%), most members of the PMC (56.7%) favored policies designed to keep down inflation. As in the 1960s and 1970s, such competing predilections posed real challenges to policymakers and state managers. Thus, the state itself became a key player in the production of political alienation and dissatisfaction.

The next chapter examines what role the state itself plays in producing political alienation among people from different classes and class layers.

establishes that pol diffs >> others, for new layer vs PMC. But the big diff is working for gov't vs private sector. Is this interesting? is the difference theorized?

Chapter Three

Class Interests and State Actions: Profiles of the Class Layers

The state plays an active part in determining the development and outcome of class struggle. It plays a central role in stabilizing society by securing the loyalty of its citizens. In the United States, the state is able to garner the loyalty and support of its citizenry, in large part, because it is able to engender and reinforce the idea that its actions are legitimate and in the interest of the nation as a whole. Such legitimacy is not a given, however. On occasion, the state has had to rely on repression, coercion, intimidation, and the inducement of fear to control groups that have posed serious challenges to its ability to govern. (Histories of the labor movement, the struggles of racial minorities, and social change efforts are filled with examples of such tactics.) Nevertheless, on most occasions, the state has not needed to resort to physical force or coercion to guarantee obedience to its rules; rather, it has been able to rely on its "legitimacy."

The state is both an actor in and product of class struggle. Although the role of the state in advanced capitalist societies has received much attention in recent years, there is a great deal of debate about the exact nature of the capitalist state and the political process in contemporary America. Disputes center around whether the state is primarily a tool of the capitalist class, an umpire that reconciles diverse interests and conflicts, or an independent entity with organizational needs and priorities of its own. Such a debate becomes relevant to any discussion about the legitimacy of America's political institutions insofar as the state as an umpire is viewed as legitimate and the state as a tool of one factions of the citizenry is viewed as illegitimate. Other things being equal, one would expect that to the extent that America's political institutions promote and facilitate the interests of one segment (especially a minority) at the expense of others, the state would have problems with maintaining the legitimacy of its political process (at least among those whose interests are not being served). From this, one might also expect the state and its political institutions to face questions of legitimacy to the extent that they openly reinforce the interests of only one segment of the society.

In this regard, several social scientists have portrayed the actions of the U.S. state as anything but legitimate (e.g., O'Connor 1973; Szyzmanski 1978; E. O. Wright 1979; Miliband 1969). These scholars have characterized America's state apparatus as a "capitalist state," which by definition functions most immediately in the interest of the capitalist class. Nevertheless, these critics of the American power structure, too, have conceded that the state does not use blatant coercion to bring about obedience. Rather, they argue that the state is able to obscure its capitalist class bias, and thus is able to dominate through "hegemony"—domination through consent, which is produced and disseminated through the political, legal, and ideological apparatuses of a society that structure the normative relationships in that society (see, e.g., Lukacs 1971; Gramsci 1971; Burawoy 1979).

Capitalist hegemony, however, is not a given. It requires that economic relations be mystified. Several formulations argue that when economic relations are demystified, changes in other spheres, including the political and ideological (superstructural), follow. Economic catastrophes, for example, are said to reveal the true class nature of the state. Such conditions make it virtually impossible for the state to rely on hegemony alone because fundamental questions about the role of the state in the economic sphere emerge. These questions politicize otherwise taken-for-granted economic arrangements and thus hinder the state's ability to legitimate from below.

Of immediate concern here is the issue of what role the capitalist state itself plays in generating class-differentiated political alienation and discontent with political policies and outcomes.

THE POLITICAL PROCESS UNDER CAPITALISM

Conflict is an integral component of the political process in America. Valued goods, rewards, and resources are finite, scarce, and unequally distributed among various groups in the society. The scarcity of these goods and resources inevitably generates conflicts over how they are to be distributed. The ultimate distribution of society's goods and resources can be explained by the existence of power differentials and the ability of groups to realize their interests by domination and social control over other groups. Even in those relationships where "authority" is thought to be the binding force, authority itself must be based ultimately on the ability of those with power to enforce their decisions through the use of coercion or other negative sanctions when necessary. Understanding politics, therefore, requires examination of group interests that lead to division and conflict, domination and exploitation, coercion and manipulation, and other means of social control. Moreover, it calls for an awareness of the fact that what often appears to be consensus is, in actuality, conformity to subordinate roles that are defined by those who are able to make their definitions binding. In short, how the society's scarce goods and resources are distributed is determined in large part by the ability of a given group to dominate or overcome the domination of other groups with conflicting interests and goals. In uncovering true political relations, the analyst has to look beyond the formal political arena to explain how it is that groups with conflicting interests have their interests realized or denied.

Beyond basic agreement about the centrality of conflict, there is much dispute about some rather key issues relevant to the political process and the determination of political outcomes even among those who see dissonance as central to the political process. There are (at least) three distinguishable models of how political outcomes come about: (1) the instrumental elite model; (2) the structuralist model; and (3) the class-coalitional model. Though these models offer a fair amount of complementarity to each other (especially when compared with consensus-based models of politics), they are in disagreement on a number of issues of importance.

One area of disagreement has to do with the degree to which the state is directly controlled by a particular class or segment of the society. Proponents of the instrumental elite model have claimed that the state is an instrument manipulated by the capitalist class in order to facilitate their class interests (e.g., Domhoff 1979; Mills 1956; Miliband 1977). They, more than other conflict-based theorists, subscribe to the view that the "modern state is but a committee for managing the affairs of the whole bourgeoisie" (Marx and Engels 1978, p. 82). Structuralists, in contrast, argue that the state has relative autonomy from the domination of the capitalist class (e.g., O'Connor 1973; E. O. Wright 1979; Wolfe 1974). They argue that this does not mean that the state does not serve the interests of capitalists, but that it is not controlled by capitalists in a direct manner. Finally, champions of the class-coalition view argue that the state is controlled by state managers (e.g., Gamson 1975; Tilly

1978). They argue that political outcomes are, to a great extent, determined by the ability of various contending and conflicting groups to convince state managers to act in their behalf.

Such a debate becomes relevant to any discussion about levels of support for America's political institutions. To the extent that America's political institutions promote and facilitate the interests of the capitalist class at the expense of others, the state has problems with maintaining its legitimacy among those whose interests are not being served. From this, one would expect the state and its political institutions to face questions of political support to the extent that they openly promote, facilitate, and reinforce the interests of the capitalist class.

What do the different visions of politics in America suggest about class-based changes in political alienation? Because these perspectives agree, at least to some extent, that feelings of political alienation reflect the discrepancies between class interests and the actions of the state, they would all suggest that it is important to identify class interests and to examine changes in state policies. When there is a high congruence between the interests of a class and the policies of the state, members of that class should be less politically alienated; conversely, when there is a large discrepancy between interests and state actions, levels of political alienation should be high.

CAPITALIST CLASS INTERESTS AND STATE ACTIONS

Because of their command of resources, capitalists are able to exercise preponderant influence on the political process. Their mechanisms of influence include such activities as making campaign contributions, lobbying, threatening "capital strikes," and controlling information. These avenues of influence are fairly universally acknowledged to exist. In theory, most of these processes are available to other segments of the society. However, capitalists are more able to use them than other groups because of their superior resources.

A second mechanism of disproportionate influence by capitalists involves the control that the capitalist class exercises over the ideological apparatus of the society, such as the media. Given that the media are large enterprises that depend on entrepreneurs for their advertising revenues, they are used to create a climate of opinion conducive to the realization of capitalist interests. Such a climate comes about not so much through direct ideological manipulation, but rather through affecting the consciousness of the public, as in reinforcing such values as competition, materialism, and individualism. The resources available to the capitalist class, then, are used not only to influence the political process directly, but also to create an ideological atmosphere that is supportive of capitalist interests and ideas.

The wealthy can also bring about their policy preferences because the very way in which the institutions of the state are structured biases the state toward the pursuit of dominant class interests. There are several structural aspects of the state that ensure it will be responsive to large employers rather than workers: the appointment rather than election of administrators; insulation of the state bureaucracy from popular control; relatively high pay to state administrators (to ensure that they identify with the wealthy rather than the poor); separation of the legislative and administrative functions of the state (to prevent any mass participation in administration where much of the real power of the state resides); and the ability of major corporations and capitalistic enterprises to make policy decisions without any meaningful input from the citizenry.

A final factor in the congruence between capitalist interests and state actions is the notion that interests of the state and state managers correspond to those of the propertied. The state under capitalism identifies with the interests of capitalists because to do otherwise imperils the economy through the loss of confidence on the part of investors. With a decline in the economy, tax revenues of the state decline and thus state resources decline. Also, a decline in the economy creates bad economic times, which are then blamed on incumbents who run the risk of being voted out of office. The ultimate outcome of this situation is that capitalist interests become identified not only as the interests of the state, but also as the national interests.

Nevertheless, even with state policies so decisively slanted toward the capitalist class, there are a number of reasons for members of the dominant class to express dissatisfactions with the political institutions of the state. First, a number of capitalists are wary of the state because of the democratic and popular-control tenets and doctrines on which the political institutions are supposedly based. These capitalists are fundamentally untrusting of institutions that—if they were *actually* democratic and operated in accordance with the needs and will of the majority—would undermine capitalist privilege. In other words, some members of the capitalist class become politically alienated from the political institutions of the state because these institutions are, or at least provide the potential for becoming, too democratic and anticapitalist.

Second, members of the capitalist class experience the policy outputs of the state as individuals. Thus, each capitalist is able to see himself as an individual rather than as a member of a powerful class that usually gets policies that reflect its general interests. As individuals who benefit from specific policies, these people need not see government actions in a class context, especially when they are able to rationalize and tell themselves that the society in general benefits. For them, such policies appear rationally based; it is only when policies potentially benefit other classes to the detriment of capitalists that they see a class bias. But as individuals, they will at times feel powerless and politically alienated. Moreover, because there are internal divisions, idiosyncrasies, varying levels of success, and other differences within the capitalist class, it is unlikely that any given person will realize his particularized interests at all times.

A third reason that capitalists might feel politically alienated is that incumbents of the state bureaucracy, who are charged with implementing state policies, are not typically members of the capitalist class. They are not members of the same networks as capitalists, nor are they from the same kinds of backgrounds. These circumstances introduce unknowns, foster capitalist hostility and distrust toward bureaucrats, and will even lead some capitalists to feel that they have no meaningful input into the political process and that the occupants of the state apparatus are unresponsive to them.

Finally, expressing discontent with government policies from time to time is a useful political strategy for capitalists. As Domhoff (1983) points out, doing so puts state managers on the defensive. It also ensures that political officials will continue to provide capitalists with signs that they are friendly to capitalist interests and that they will try to be accommodating. So that capitalist abeyance will not be mistaken as apathy by policymakers, especially when other classes are articulating their interests, it is necessary from time to time for capitalists to make known their discontentment with the direction of state policies. In short, political alienation among the capitalist class, just like alienation among the other classes and class fractions, reflects not only objective discrepancies between interests and state actions, but also subjective interpretations of such discrepancies, posturing, and uncertainties about those who make and implement state policies.

POLITICAL ALIENATION AMONG NONCAPITALISTS

Under capitalism, the state has a capitalist bias. By definition, a capitalist state exists in order to facilitate the perceived interests of the capitalist class as a whole. Under such a mandate there is a natural tendency toward entropy with respect to its relations with other noncapitalist classes. It experiences difficulties in its attempts to garner the support of those classes whose interests it negates in its attempts to provide abutments for capital. In light of its capitalist class bias, were the state to do nothing to secure the support of the professional-managerial class, the new layer, the traditional working class, and the poor, it would have extreme difficulty in securing the support of these noncapitalists. By the same token, to the extent that the state actively and aggressively promotes the interests of capital to the detriment of these class fractions, it must successfully define capitalist interests as the "national" (i.e., neutral, unbiased) interests, compensate for its biases by offering the working class something in return, or run the risk having its levels of support among working-class citizens undermined.

Under ordinary circumstances, the state offers social welfare and entitlement programs to the different factions of the working class in return for their tolerance of its pro-capitalist policies. It offers relatively higher social reward when there is a greater potential challenge to its decision making prerogatives or for disruption of its routines. Accordingly, as the potential for challenge or disruption becomes greater, there is a tendency toward higher social wages, more autonomy in the workplace, lower rates of exploitation of labor power, and lower rates of tax exploitation. To the degree that the various working-class fractions pose different challenges to the state's decision making, it offers different kinds of inducements to appease them (or comminations to intimidate them). Thus, the class fractions' reactions to the state's policies differ, at times, to the point of running counter to each other.

It is worth reiterating here that the capitalist class is not all-powerful. Nor is the state always capable of acting in the interest of capital. Power in American society is not as one-sided as portrayed by the instrumental elite model of the political process. Different class coalitions may wrest control of the legislature and determine the direction and content of state policies. Coalitions of underdog groups can gain electoral control and force state managers to enact policies that are more in line with their interests. The electoral process, therefore, is not unimportant. Through coalitions, it can be used as a mode of class struggle to gain those victories for the working class, which no longer may be attainable through struggles on the shop floor. Such class-based actions force the state's hand and undermine its claims of being neutral and unbiased. They also limit the options available to state managers and thereby make it more likely that the state will have to make policy choices that hurt particular classes and class fractions. These choices differentially affect class fractions and thus differentially affect their levels of political alienation.

By their very nature, however, coalitions are fragile. They depend on grass-roots participation. Groups will enter into them only under certain structural conditions (e.g., when they feel that their interests are at stake and cannot be attained as efficiently without cooperating with others). In the absence of coalitions among working-class fractions, the capitalist class will win virtually all contests. Unfettered, the state under capitalism has a "natural" tendency to protect the interests of capital and to be unresponsive to the needs and interests of noncapitalists. Not surprisingly, the levels of political distrust and alienation among non-capitalists rises in direct proportion to the degree that the state pursues capitalist class interests to the detriment of the interests of their specific class fraction. In other words, there are some more particular reasons why the various working-class fractions experience their conditions under capitalism as alienating. These are discussed below.

The Professional-Managerial Class

For millions of Americans in the professional-managerial class, the early 1960s were the last halcyon days in America. Though this period included high levels of civil rights movement activity, the assassination of John F. Kennedy, and the beginnings of the Vietnam War, this era was the last point in time before the state became involved in actions that this class fraction would see as assaults on their immediate interests. As demonstrated in Chapter 4, for the next quarter of a century, levels of political alienation among this stratum were to increase virtually without interruption. These increases in alienation for this mostly conservative portion of the middle layers can be linked to their dissatisfaction with the state's handling of a number of issues and causes that grew out of the 1960s. In particular, the PMC experienced increases in their levels of political alienation due to trends toward proletarianization of their work, threats to their life-styles, growing competition with capital, the state, and the traditional working class for suzerainty in the workplace, and shifting tax burdens that made them more responsible for providing the financial wherewithal for subsidies to both the wealthy and the poor.

Levels of political alienation among members of the professional-managerial class tended to increase to the degree that they felt that the state was aiding and abetting those who sought to undermine their life-styles and culture. Most members of the PMC felt the government sided with progressives and other countercultural elements that grew out of the 1960s who wanted to change Americans' predilection toward inequality, "technological advancements," materialism, and so forth. Policies such as affirmative action, bussing, and the Great Society programs were not explicitly class-based in nature, but they did challenge cherished values of the more conservative faction of the middle layers. To members of the PMC, those policies were affronts to their middle-class values and, thus, were class-based causes of political alienation.

The professional-managerial class's ability to identify and establish a cultural and political niche for themselves was not only challenged in the general society, but also in the workplace. When government policy began requiring equal employment opportunities and affirmative action, not only did managers feel that it took away some of their discretion, but also it changed the cultural mix of their environments by including previously excluded groups. Again, these policies were perceived as attacks on freedom of choice and other "American" values, and they tended to raise the levels of political alienation among those layers who saw the government as playing an active role in bringing about such changes.

These changes brought on by the state were compounded by the actions of capitalists. With the ascendence of foreign competition and the notion that "foreign models" would enhance productivity, capitalists pushed their corporate managers to incorporate the ideas of the Japanese and Europeans into their management techniques. These changes toward quality circles, for example, meant more "workplace democracy," which again meant less control over the labor process for managers. These changes also meant the imposition of new cultural norms and types on professionals and managers who were more or less accustomed to defining what were appropriate behaviors on the shop floor and in the corporation.

Professionals and managers experienced other setbacks in their discretion that increased their levels of political alienation, but also had less to do with the direct actions of the state and more to do with the conduct of capitalists. As Wright and Singlemann (1982) suggest, there has been a tendency toward proletarianization of the labor process, that is, the removal of skill and discretion from workers with autonomy. They go on to document empirically that, between 1960 and 1970, "the routinization of activity [became] more and more pervasive, extending to technical and even professional occupations; and responsibilities within work [became] less meaningful" (Wright and Singlemann 1982, p. S178). These actions, though aimed at enhancing the capitalists' degree of social control and increasing rates of productivity, had the more general effect of deepening alienation among professional and technical workers.

As professional workers were increasingly losing battles over their autonomy in the workplace, the state was engaging in policies that increased the rate of tax exploitation foisted upon this layer. The mid–1960s through the 1980s were years of high inflation. Though inflation had previously played little part in raising or shifting tax burdens, by 1965 it pushed PMC taxpayers into higher tax brackets without increasing their real incomes. This bracket creep, in addition to the redistribution of tax burdens away from commercial and industrial property toward residential property that occurred during the period, led to larger tax bills and lower real incomes for professionals and managers. Even worse from the PMC's perspective, these higher taxes made it more possible for a larger public sector to exist. Needless to say, these actions generally raised levels of alienation among the PMC, as they felt that their tax dollars were being used to support the very groups who were attempting to undermine them and their way of life.

In sum, the state played both direct and indirect roles in increasing levels of political alienation among members of the professional-managerial class.

The New Layer

Many of the same issues that sparked increases in political alienation among members of the professional-managerial class were responsible for raising levels of alienation among members of the new layer. The state's handling of the aftereffects of the 1960s, routinization of their work, competition with other class fractions over life-styles and cultural issues, and the state's mismanagement of taxation and economic policies were all sources that elevated levels of alienation for the new layer, just as they did for the PMC. In many instances, however, the state's policies hiked political disaffection for both class segments, but for diametrically opposed reasons. State policies that were too progressive for the PMC often were too conservative for the more meliorist members of the new layer, and vice versa. The new layer, though similar to members of the PMC in terms of living-standard and background characteristics, experienced many of the policies of the state as alienating because they were more likely to identify with underdog groups and to hold policy preferences that were consistent with the interests of such groups. This is not to suggest that such choices were purely altruistic, however. Quite to the contrary, the new layer—many of whom worked in the state sector providing services to underdog groups—developed political interests that paralleled those of less privileged working-class fractions. To the degree that new-layer interests overlapped with those of underdog groups, their levels of political alienation climbed when the state took actions that were deleterious to such groups.

The successes of the civil rights movement and the expansion of antipoverty and Great Society programs bode greater opportunity for blacks, the poor, and other underdog groups. But on another level, underdog group demands for access and opportunity translated into tangible benefits for those in the new layer. Items on the liberal agenda meant additional opportunities for new-layer liberals themselves. Expansion of social welfare programs led to greater demand for social workers and other social service employees. New community programs signaled more funding for those with the appropriate credentials. Increased access to education enhanced the need for educators in the public schools, and extra demand for instructors and professors in the college ranks.

Such positions allowed members of the new layer to increase their importance and visibility in the society. They provided a means for the new layer to put into practice many of the ideals that they espoused and cherished. With the sizable increase in people-oriented programs, members of the new layer were able to feel as though they were providing meaningful service to their fellow human beings. At the same time, they were getting paid for doing good. They were able to put their imprints on the cultural value system of the nation. More importantly, they were able to reproduce themselves by expanding their ranks and by making more room for others with the same outlooks.

During the mid 1970s the state started retrenching on programs that had allowed the new layer to flourish. These actions challenged the new layer on several fronts and had many effects on them, most of which led to higher levels of alienation. Most immediately, the state's change in priorities affected the new layer on their jobs. As cost-cutting measures, state managers reduced the rate of growth and budgets for programs that employed many of these new-layer workers. In addition, they often called for the implementation of new work rules, policies, and procedures that curtailed the autonomy of public sector workers. And they set government-spending priorities such that workers in this sector would receive pay increases that did not keep pace with increases in their cost of living.

More important to many in the new layer, however, was their decreased ability to re-create the society in their image. In the absence of movement activity and underdog group allies, new-layer workers were vulnerable to the whims of the state, which was by far their largest employer. New-layer employees became expendable. When the state's agenda changed, cutbacks ensued. With cutbacks in social programs, not only did new-layer workers lose jobs, but also they lost influence over the direction and priorities of the society. With fewer positions available to them, they were not as able to promote their progressive agenda. In fact, as the tide of public opinion and government action turned away from humanistic concerns and people programs, state bureaucrats, educators, social workers, and other state sector employees became the icons of everything that was wrong with liberalism, social programs, and the government. Increasingly they came under attack but had few mechanisms to protect themselves. Obviously, their levels of alienation reflected those occurrences.

In addition to these alienating experiences, the state's bungling of tax policies and the economy left members of the new layer with even higher levels of political alienation. Members of the new layer did not complain about taxes going to support programs for the poor and other underdog groups as did the PMC. Rather, they protested that the wealthy were not paying their fair share. These middle-layer progressives understood that a great deal of government expenditures went toward supporting business interests and corporate welfare programs. They were upset with inflationary policies that robbed them of their incomes, especially when changes in the cost of living outpaced their pay raises and left even less real income after taxes. They scowled at high unemployment rates, not only because such problems affected them personally, but also because such situations displaced others about whom they were genuinely concerned. The new layer was concerned about all of these issues during the heyday of movement activities. As economic recessions became more frequent and severe, and as the state's fiscal and economic policies relegated growing proportions of the populace into financial distress, these concerns became wariness. Consequently, as government cut back on programs that were important to the new layer and implemented policies that hurt them and those they cared about, their levels of political alienation climbed steadily.

The Traditional Working Class

As with all other classes and class fractions, members of the traditional working class are shaped by their relationship to the means of production. As "hired help," traditional workers sell their labor power in order to endure. Unlike their new layer and PMC brethren, however, members of the traditional working class are usually involved in physically demanding, strenuous "dirty work." Their jobs are often boring and physically exhausting. More importantly, jobs for the traditional working class are often debasing and disallow opportunities for retention of dignity. The workers who hold such jobs occupy mid-level to low positions within the occupational structure. Their occupations are characterized by relatively low skill levels, fewer educational requirements, and lower degrees of task complexity. Their jobs usually involve manual labor and include little autonomy.

There are, however, some distinctions within the traditional working class. Some of these workers have skilled jobs that require training, are better paying, and provide security. Others demand fewer skills, are less rewarding both materially and psychologically, and are more subject to the vagaries of the economy or the whims of employers. Generally, workers' positions in the occupational structure are related to other aspects of their social lives. Such positions not only affect how these workers fare economically, but also influence how others view these workers and how they view themselves.

Because most traditional workers tend to occupy low positions in bureaucratic authority structures, they take orders from many layers above and are seldom in positions to give orders to others. They are told what to do at work, how it should be done, and when and how fast it should be done. For the most part, such workers have lost control over the process of production. As a consequence, they are alienated from their labor power, and their work activity no longer has intrinsic meaning to them. Work has become alienating to them and has become only a means of subsisting.

Alienating conditions in the sphere of work have consequences in other realms. Alienation in work often segments other aspects of their lives. Work becomes something to be tolerated. Traditional workers "sell pieces of themselves in order to try to buy them back each night and weekend with the coin of 'fun' " (Mills 1951, p. 237). Life becomes departmentalized to such an extent that most workers take the perspective that there are hours for work, and there are hours away from work.

Perhaps the most important and relevant consequences of alienation in the workplace manifest themselves in the political arena. For example, studies have consistently shown a strong relationship between conditions in the world of work and political ideology, partisanship, and participation (e.g., Knoke and Hout 1974; Hamilton 1972; Levinson 1975). Members of the traditional working class tend to vote for liberal political parties, to think of themselves as democrats, and to abstain from the formal political process altogether.

Members of the traditional working class face relatively higher costs of participating in the formal political process (Piven and Cloward 1988). Registration laws (which are a disservice to workers), lack of direct access to policymakers, inadequate discretional time and resources, and a dearth of political figures who actually would represent true working-class interests, all lead to low levels of political involvement. In addition, political alienation, which tends to be higher among members of the traditional working class, further deflates their involvement.

Because the political system is so stacked against traditional workers' interests, and because these workers are so alienated in their workplace, their levels of political alienation are not very elastic. Their levels of disaffection are not as subject to fluctuation for political and economic causes as are those of the new layer and the PMC. Levels of political alienation among such workers are not constant, but they do tend to be overwhelmed by other considerations that also affect political propensities.

For traditional workers, alienation, humiliation, and dignity denial on the job can lead to higher levels of working-class consciousness, politicization of class-based deprivations, and political activism. As is true for other groups, when traditional workers recognize that they have strong class interests that can be achieved through collective efforts, they will work together to pursue their common interests. More often, however, such collective interests are not apprehended. As a result, traditional workers tend to resort to more individualistic responses such as higher rates of absenteeism on the job, higher rates of quitting and dismissal, sabotage, defiance, and so on. Unfortunately, however, attempts at dealing with these negative experiences and states also take on such forms as hostilities directed toward minority groups, student radicals on college campuses, and others who are perceived as threats. For these reasons, members of the traditional working class often are not as progressive in their political orientations as one might anticipate. They are not, however, as reactionary as they are often portrayed in the popular media. Nevertheless, their short- and medium-run interests do not necessarily coincide with those of the new layer nor the PMC. Thus, their patterns of change in political alienation do not parallel those of the new layer nor the PMC.

The Poor

The poor have few or no opportunities for economic initiative, decision making, or control over their lives. For the most part, these members of the working class are faced with limited options. Virtually all aspects of their social spheres are mandated by external sources. Social life for these impoverished workers is highly restricted to intermittent work, family, and the local community organizations.

The jobs available to and filled by the poor are those that demand the fewest skills and experience, carry the least responsibility, and pay the lowest wages. By definition, this underprivileged fraction of the working class holds marginal kinds of employment or no jobs at all. When they are employed, such workers have little reason to feel more than a casual and temporary commitment to the tasks that they perform. Their jobs provide no meaningful opportunities for promotion or upward mobility. Nor do they grant many occasions to develop long-term commitments among such workers. Consequently, the poor feel and express dissatisfaction with most aspects of their jobs.

The poor are a product of the logic of capitalism, which requires a low-wage sector in order to apply downward pressures on wages. Like others in the working class, they are, to a large extent, at the mercy of those who own the means of production. Unlike others in the working class, however, the poor are located almost exclusively at the bottom of the economic authority structure. Those with jobs give orders to virtually no one. They work under extremely woeful conditions. They generally receive degraded treatment. And they are unceasingly subject to humiliation.

Untold numbers of the poor are excluded from the system altogether. They depend on the welfare state for their subsistence. Some are retired workers whose labor has been maximally exploited. Others are former employees who have been physically or psychologically injured. Some have no skills or characteristics that capital finds exploitable. And still others simply refuse to submit their talents and labor to capital for the price that is offered.

It could be argued that the existence of the excluded poor is also an outgrowth of capitalism. Just as the working poor serve to undercut wages, the excluded poor act as a reference point to exhort the working poor to continue to put up with their lot in order to avoid the status of being on the dole. Indeed, because being poor in America is viewed so negatively, the poor themselves often explain their own status in individualist, self-blaming terms, despite their first-hand knowledge of structural barriers.

Not surprisingly, the poor do not feel as powerful as other segments of the society. They do not feel that they have control over their own fates. These reality-based feelings are as true of the political arena as they are of other realms. Traditional avenues of power and influence are all but closed off to the poor. To the degree that the true interests of the poor are antithetical to those of the wealthy and other clout-wielding groups, it is unlikely that ordinary politics will bring about policies that qualitatively improve the fortunes of the poor. They have few of the traditional means of political influence; thus, their needs and druthers are usually ignored.

When the poor resort to revolts, when they threaten the social order, or use other unruly political strategies, their situation changes somewhat. However, politics by other means are not very common. As Piven and Cloward (1977, p. 7) so eloquently point out, it is "only under exceptional conditions . . . [that] the lower classes [are] afforded the socially determined opportunity to press for their own class interests." So ordinarily, the policy preferences of the poor go unaddressed. Consequently, their levels of political alienation are typically higher than those of other class fractions.

With outbreaks of riots and other civil disturbances, however, welfare rolls expanded by more than 100 percent during the 1960s (Piven and Cloward 1971). The welfare benefits in major cities that experienced riots grew much more rapidly than did those in cities where no disorders occurred (Betz 1974). And those locations that weathered the most severe and frequent riots realized the largest growths in welfare benefits (Isaac and Kelly 1981). Clearly, welfare benefits were used as a means of appeasing the rebellious poor who dared to challenge the status quo. Such strategies had the desired effects of "cooling out" the poor and slowing down their rates of increase in political alienation. Nevertheless, these policies did not reduce levels of political alienation among the poor, as state managers might have hoped.

Chapter Four

Class-Based Changes in Political Alienation: Political Disaffection Perspectives

During the past quarter of a century, America's political system has lost a great deal of public support and confidence. These declines are well-documented. For example, according to survey results from the Center for Political Studies' National Election Surveys (CPS-NES), in 1964 more than three out of four Americans (76%) expressed the belief that they could "trust the government in Washington to do what [was] right" just about all of the time or at least some of the time. By 1980, however, only one out of four (25%) trusted the government to do what was right. Similarly, in 1964 nearly two of three Americans (64%) believed that their government was "run for the benefit of all people." This proportion had dropped to about one in five (21%) in 1980. During the 1970s, over half of the American voting-age population (51%) came to believe that their public officials did not care much what people like them thought. These declines in support and confidence are well-documented in the "political disaffection" literature on political alienation and political legitimacy (e.g., Miller 1983; Macke 1979; Hibbs et al. 1982; House and Mason 1975). Indeed, these drops in confidence and trust were so pronounced in the late 1970s that social scientists, political analysts, and government leaders proclaimed that America was in the midst of a "crisis of confidence" (e.g., Caddell 1979; Miller 1983).

The "political disaffection" literature has provided several formulations to explain why some Americans believe that their government, political leaders, policymakers, and political institutions are uncaring, unresponsive, inattentive, and untrustworthy. These explanations agree on a set of core issues. They do vary, however, in what they see as the causes of fluctuations in political alienation.

Surprisingly—especially for an era that witnessed the civil rights movement, the Vietnam War, and the assassination of a president— research revealed that "shifts in [political] alienation . . . [had] occurred remarkably uniformly across demographic groups" (House and Mason 1975, p. 126) through the 1950s and 1960s. These trends and patterns in political alienation did change. But even today, despite the dramatic, well-documented increases in levels and rates of political alienation, some of these prominent theoretical formulations would lead one to believe that these increases are not, or at least *should not* be, occurring. Other formulations, though not so blatantly inaccurate, still would lead one astray in terms of understanding the bases and sources of class-based changes in political alienation. The prevailing wisdom among these formulations is that changes have been more rapid among people with memberships in groups with low structural locations or that such changes have been (at the very least) virtually uniform in all subpopulations. Neither of these has been the case.

Existing theoretical explanations of cross-sectional and longitudinal variations in levels of subjective political alienation fall into three broad types. They can be termed (1) spirit of the times theories; (2) political culture and socialization theories; and (3) political structure and interest group theories. These explanations do not explicitly link variations in political alienation to the operation of the state under capitalism. Nor do they examine the role that the state plays in struggles existing in the society. Therefore, they are limited in varying degrees in their ability to pinpoint the underlying forces that drive political alienation in the society.

This chapter examines political disaffection explanations of declines in support for and confidence in the political institutions of America from 1964 through 1980. In doing so, it outlines three models of "political alienation" (the general term this literature uses to refer to feelings of discontent directed toward the political institutions of the state) that are consistent with and representative of the political disaffection perspective. Further, this chapter presents empirical evidence that bears on these explanations of change in political alienation in order to test three variants of this model that make different predictions about patterns of change in political alienation. It demonstrates that, while these theories sound plausible and provide some insight into the patterns of change in political trust and efficacy, they are at best incomplete formulations that would not lead one to anticipate important trends in political alienation. Data analysis indicates that political personality, culture, and socialization explanations—variants of this approach—do not account for

close to the meub of his argument

the patterns of change in political alienation. Further, results show that, contrary to the hypotheses posed by explanations that predict uniform changes in levels of political alienation for all groups in the society, there were significant variations in patterns of change in levels of political alienation. Many of the results are consistent with the political interest group formulation that predicts differential changes in levels of political alienation; nevertheless, much remains to be explained.

POLITICAL CULTURE AND SOCIALIZATION THEORIES

Political culture and socialization theories are part of a broader class of culture and personality explanations that view attitudes and person- ality traits as relatively stable and enduring personal dispositions ac- quired early in life through experiences in the family, school, and social milieu in which a person grows up. Proponents have not always ex- amined these characteristics for the same reasons. Some social research- ers have used these sociodemographic characteristics primarily as variables that had to be statistically controlled when examining the re- lationship between political alienation and variables other than sociod- emographics (e.g., Kluegel et al. 1977); others have used them, at times only implicitly, as surrogates for political personalities, political social- ization, or political culture (e.g., Almond and Verba 1963; J. D. Wright 1976). Thus, the emphases in these studies have differed and the results from the various studies, using various samples and operationalizations of political alienation, have not been in agreement over the effects of these characteristics on political alienation. Nevertheless, it is possible to summarize the general propositions offered by proponents of this sociodemographic approach, and thus, it is possible to determine whether this approach would lead one to expect uniform or differential rates of change in patterns of political alienation.

Social scientists who have used sociodemographic factors primarily as variables that had to be statistically controlled when examining the re- lationship between political alienation and variables other than socio- demographics generally have included such factors for implicit rather than explicit theoretical reasons. Kluegel et al. (1977) offer a good ex- ample of this practice. In their study, they correlated respondents' levels of political alienation with their personal and demographic character- istics not because they were interested in how these variables related to political alienation per se, but rather because they were interested in determining the net effects of political alienation on subjective class identification. In other words, they developed a statistical model that specified several sociodemographic factors as prior variables that are associated with political alienation, which in turn facilitates (or hinders, depending on the level of alienation) class identification. In terms of

explaining the relationships between the sociodemographic variables
and political alienation, Kluegel et al. failed to make the links between
the correlations they observed and the underlying theoretical reasons
for these correlations (though they provided ample rationale for the
relationship between political alienation and class identification, which
was the relationship of primary concern in the study). They included
the sociodemographic variables primarily to act as statistical controls.

By way of contrast, social scientists who have included sociodemographic variables in their analyses as surrogates for political personality
traits have done so because they believe such factors have theoretically
meaningful effects on political alienation. In general,

[P]ersonality is used as a generic label for relatively stable and enduring individual psychological attributes (values, attitudes, motives, needs, beliefs, etc.).
. . . Personality often connotes something more distinctive than any or all per-
sisting psychological attributes of an individual. . . . [I]t suggests that these attributes have a structure or organization and some inherent dynamic properties
or tendencies (House 1981, p. 4).

Political personality proponents posit that political alienation is a
"learned, generalized world view that encompasses a sense of powerlessness, strain, and self-estrangement" (Mirowsky and Ross 1983,
p. 229). It is related to the "cognitive habit of interpreting the intentions
and behaviors of others as unsupportive, self-seeking, and devious"
(Mirowsky and Ross 1983, p. 229). Because these personality traits "are
associated with one's socioeconomic position and ethnicity" (Mirowsky
and Ross 1983, p. 228), this body of research argues that life in certain
sociodemographic positions is characterized by feelings of distrust, powerlessness, and victimization—key components of alienation according
to this approach.

Proponents of this perspective do not necessarily agree on the reasons
why sociodemographics are related to political alienation. Some researchers, pointing to cultural factors, emphasize the "national" and
"community" character in which the individual's identity is derived.
They often point to the "pathological" characteristics of one's social
environment, which lead to paranoia, anomia, authoritarianism, alienation, and other forms of maladjustment. They indicate that such mal-
adjustments occur most frequently among those with low social status.
For these analysts, alienation is not necessarily a reflection of reality; it
is, however, a personality trait found among those who have trouble
adjusting to the stresses and strains of everyday life.

Other researchers, pointing to the objective conditions in which the
various sociodemographic groups live, note that people in lower status
groups are more likely to be victims and thus have more reason to

develop personalities that include feelings of powerlessness, distrust, and cynicism (e.g., Campbell et al. 1976; Grabb 1979; Mirowsky and Ross 1983); thus, these groups have higher levels of alienation in general and higher levels of political alienation in particular. For these social scientists, alienation is a reflection and direct result of the objective conditions in which one lives. In other words, political personality proponents vary in their beliefs about why certain sociodemographic characteristics result in political personality traits that are supposedly related to political alienation. However, they do agree on the notion that sociodemographic characteristics are related to personality traits that either give rise to political alienation or include political alienation (as one of the traits). Moreover, they generally agree that "low-status" groups have higher concentrations of the personality traits that lead to or include political alienation.

A final related body of research derives more from theoretical formulations about "political culture" and "political socialization." Proponents of this approach also use sociodemographic variables as surrogates for concepts that they attempt to relate to political alienation. Fortunately, the fit between their data and theories is generally much better than that attained by those making arguments about personalities and political alienation. Unfortunately for this perspective, however, most of the theorizing has been implicit rather than explicit. Also, when explanations about differences in political culture that produce differential levels and rates of political alienation and other attitudinal differences have been put forth, these "[e]xplanations . . . [have been] vague, posthoc, and also never explicitly tested" (House 1981, p. 28). Nevertheless, by examining the basic tenets of this perspective, it is possible to derive some propositions and determine a priori what this approach would lead one to expect with respect to differences in political alienation by sociodemographic categories.

House (1981, p. 34) defines "culture" as "a set of cognitive and evaluative beliefs—beliefs about what is or what ought to be—that are shared by the members of a social system and transmitted to new members." Relatedly, "political culture . . . refers to the specifically political orientations—attitudes toward the political system and its various parts, and attitudes toward the role of the self in the system" (Almond and Verba 1963, p. 13). Social scientists who offer "political culture" and "political socialization" explanations of differential levels and rates political alienation "see group differences . . . (between nations, races, social classes, etc.) as rooted in the different beliefs and values shared within each group, which are in turn generally seen to arise from the different ways people in these groups have been socialized from early life" (House 1981, p. 33). In short, they see attitudes about the political system in general and political alienation in particular as emerging from shared

values that are learned from others in one's immediate social environment. Thus, the use of sociodemographic variables enables users of this
approach to capture the essence of "political culture group" differences.

Almond and Verba (1963), for example, maintain that political culture,
the chief determinant of political orientations in general and of political
alienation in particular, is transmitted by a process that includes both
intended and unintended training in such social institutions as the family, peer groups, the school, and the workplace. They argue that:

[I]ndividuals learn political orientations through intentional teaching, as in a
school civics class; but they also learn through overtly political experiences that
are not intended to be lessons in politics or when they observe the action of the
political system. Or the training in political orientation may be neither explicit
nor political in content, as when the individual learns about authority from
participating in authority structures in the family or the school or when he learns
about the trustworthiness of others from his early contact with adults. . . .
[O]rientations developed in childhood will be further modified by later, direct
experiences with politics. . . . [E]xpectations and norms about participation will
interact with the opportunities that the political system offers for participation,
with the importance . . . place[d] on particular issues, and with the demands
other roles place upon [the individual].

A major part of political socialization, then, involves direct exposure. . . . [E]ach
new generation absorbs [their political] culture through exposure to the political
attitudes and behaviors of the preceding generation (Almond and Verba 1963,
p. 499).

Similarly, James Wright (1976, p. 263) argues that "[p]olitical alienation originates . . . in supper-time conversation, as one of the informal
political' 'lessons' transmitted across generations in the lower and working classes." He goes on to say that "efficacy and trust . . . are not isolated
attitudes, but rather elements in entire belief configurations that characterize the various social classes" (p. 263). For him, then, political alienation is not a personality trait, but rather a cultural trait that can be
transmitted from generation to generation via the same mechanisms that
other cultural traits are transmitted.

A final variant of this genre is a perspective that makes arguments
about "working-class authoritarianism" (e.g., Lipset 1963). This view is
predicated on the belief that the masses generally lack the political virtues
and values that are necessary for successful operation of democracy.
Because of their antidemocratic orientations and predispositions, the
untrusting, uninformed, and intolerant masses pose serious challenges
to the political system. Ironically, widespread participation by these folks
leads to "negative democracy." For example, Mannheim (1940) suggests
that the participation of the masses in democratic politics actually results
in such conspicuously antidemocratic outcomes as the repression of

dissent, intolerance of minorities, and pursuit of simple-minded and short-term political solutions. The challenge to political leaders, therefore, is to govern by garnering enough political support from the masses without awakening their unrestrained participation and without encouraging their authoritarian tendencies and antidemocratic initiatives. In other words, political leaders must engender trust among the citizenry, but also they must thwart the "extremist" inclinations that often accompany these citizens' participation.

Most political personality, culture, and socialization theorists predict that political alienation will be higher for groups characterized by low socioeconomic status or positions of lower power and prestige in society. Change in levels of alienation in the population over time would be produced by: (1) changes in the composition of the population with respect to early socialization experiences; or (2) significant shifts in the nature of the socialization experiences of a generation. Rises in alienation should, for example, be a product of an increase in those kinds of people in the population who have acquired alienated attitudes early in life (e.g., the poor and working-class people). Alternatively, a process of cohort succession in which new cohorts enter adulthood with notably more alienation attitudes than prior generations can produce increases in overall levels of alienation. Since much of the culture and socialization explanations rest on processes of intergenerational transmission, change should be gradual over time and more likely to result from compositional than cohort changes.

Many social scientists rely on political culture and socialization theories of political alienation. Research on the sources of *change* in alienation has not provided much evidence for the central claims of this perspective, however. In fact, proponents of this perspective are likely to emphasize the *persistence* of one's political culture throughout the life cycle and continuity in political outlooks. Thus, they would lead one to believe that apparent changes in political alienation are statistical artifacts that disappear once one considers the compositional changes in the society, that is, once one controls for the disproportionate growth or shrinking of groups with high levels of alienation. Political alienation increases, they would argue, because the size of groups with high alienation increases (or the size of groups with low alienation decreases). Political alienation decreases because the size of groups with high alienation decreases (or the size of groups with low alienation increases). The net effect of these sociodemographic effects is that levels of political alienation remain virtually constant.

Before assessing the accuracy of this perspective, however, there are a number of concepts that must be identified and operationally defined. The meanings and operational definitions of these concepts are discussed below.

CONCEPTUALIZATIONS, OPERATIONALIZATIONS, AND METHODOLOGICAL CONSIDERATIONS

The data to be used in assessing the political disaffection model come from the University of Michigan's Survey Research Center's Center for Political Studies' National Election Surveys (CPS-NES). They are from the five presidential-election-year surveys from 1964 through 1980. The samples were national, representative cross-sectional "samples of citizens of voting age . . . living within the coterminus United States" (ICPSR 1981, cover page). Included in this study are those respondents who were interviewed both before and after the election. There were the following number of respondents in each sample: 1,834 in 1964; 1,673 in 1968; 2,705 in 1972; 2,248 in 1976; and 1,614 in 1980—a total of 10,074 respondents.[1] Data from these respondents are used to empirically assess the formulations of the political disaffection models.

Before an empirical assessment of these models can be carried out, there are a number of concepts that must be identified and operationally defined. Specifically, "period effects," "sociodemographic characteristics," and "political alienation" must be explicated. The meanings and operational definitions of these concepts are discussed below.[2]

Political Alienation

For subjective political alienation, there are two central dimensions of concern: political trust and political inefficacy. Following the work of Mason et al. (1985), subjective political alienation is operationalized with the "No Say/Don't Care" (Inefficacy) index and the "No Trust/Big Interests" (Distrust) index (Mason et al. 1985).

The No Say/Don't Care (Inefficacy) index taps beliefs about government responsiveness. It is composed of the following two statements: "People like me don't have any say about what the government does" and "I don't think public officials care much what people like me think." Respondents who disagree with both statements are given a score of one. Respondents who agree with one statement and disagree with the other are given a score of three. Respondents who agree with both statements are given a five. Thus, the index ranges from one to five, with five being the highest level of subjective political inefficacy. In order to make results more accessible, however, most scores have been multiplied by 20, and thus, range from a low of 20 to a high of 100.

The No Trust/Big Interests (Distrust) index corresponds to the trust dimension. It is made up of responses to two questions. The questions read as follows: "How often do you think you can trust the government in Washington to do what is right—just about all the time, most of the time, or only some of the time?" and "Would you say that the government is pretty much run by a few big interests looking out for themselves or that it is run for the benefit of all people?" Respondents who felt that the government could be trusted "just about all the time" were given a score of one. Those who said "most of the time" were given a score of three, and those who said "only some of the time" or none of the time were given a score of five. Respondents who said the government is "run for the benefit of all people" were given a score of one; those who said that the government is "pretty much run by a few big interests looking out for themselves" were given a score of five. The scores from the two items were added together and divided by two. The scores for the distrust index ranged from a low political distrust score of one to a high of five. Again, to make results more accessible, most scores have been multiplied by 20, and thus, range from a low of 20 to a high of 100.

The operationalizations of political alienation employed here are well-established in the empirically oriented political alienation literature. Mason et al. (1985, p. 65) argue that one "can be certain that in using this set of measures, an analyst would not miss or obscure important information regarding the nature of causes and consequences of political alienation in America." As they also point out, the widespread use of the National Election Survey items "has endowed them with quasi-theoretical status, although the measures are not derived from an explicit theory of political alienation" (p. 8).

There have been, however, a number of alternative operationalizations of subjective political alienation. Unfortunately, there has been "a strong tendency to use ad hoc measures consisting of a small number of items . . . [which are] not particularly systematic or comparable with any well-known index" (Seeman 1975, p. 94). Nevertheless, Mason et al. identify three traditions: (1) the Seeman tradition (e.g., Seeman 1959; Seeman 1972); (2) the Easton/Gamson tradition (e.g., Easton 1965; Gamson 1968a); and (3) the Michigan Survey Research Center tradition (e.g., House and Mason 1975; J. D. Wright 1976). These various approaches to operationalizing subjective political alienation are discussed below. Shortcomings peculiar to each approach are pointed out, and the limitations of these approaches as a general type are also presented.

The first tradition is associated with the work of Seeman (1959, 1972, 1975). Others (e.g., Finifter 1970) have used modified versions of Seeman's typology to examine such dimensions of political alienation as "political powerlessness," "political meaninglessness," "political normlessness," and "political isolation." Within the empirically oriented political alienation literature, however, studies that have attempted to adapt Seeman's framework have come under attack for failing to establish construct validity; that is, they generally have failed to demonstrate what is specifically political about their measures. Moreover, their measures have tended to confuse and blend in notions such as "anomie" and "locus of control," which have, at best, a tenuous relationship to the classical notion of alienation. In short, this approach runs into the danger of obscuring the objects of respondents' political alienation.

The second tradition, the Easton/Gamson tradition, "derive[s] more from analysis of problems of authority, influence, and control in political systems . . . "(Mason et al. 1985, p. 6). Social scientists working within this tradition make it a point to distinguish between "efficacy/input" dimensions and "trust/output" dimensions of political alienation. As Mason et al. (1985, p. 6) point out, those authors credited with first distinguishing between these two dimensions, Easton (1965) and Gamson (1968a) "have not identified or developed clear empirical indicators of their two dimensions of alienation, nor have they provided explicit empirical tests of the validity of the distinction." Several others, however, have employed measures that have attempted to distinguish between the trust and efficacy dimensions of political alienation (e.g., Almond and Verba 1963; Aberbach 1969; Paige 1971; Fraser 1974; Ambramson 1972), but the results across studies are not entirely consistent" (Mason et al. 1985, p. 6).

Studies operating within the third tradition, the Michigan Survey Research Center tradition, "are by far the most commonly encountered in the literature on political discontent—so common, in fact that contributions such as Gamson's were written with explicit reference to them" (J. D. Wright 1976, p. 91). By the same token, many studies using data from Michigan's Survey Research Center (SRC) have tried to approximate the dimensions of political alienation identified by the other two traditions. "Little consensus has emerged, however, on what constructs from the . . . [other two] traditions, if any, are measured by the Michigan indices" (Mason et al. 1985, p. 9).

Though some of the indicators used by those operating with the Michigan SRC tradition have been questioned for their construct validity, unlike those from the other two traditions, these measures do have the benefit of being generally recognized as valid indicators of political alienation; that is, they benefit from consensual validity. Moreover, each of the subjective political alienation indices to be used in this study has been factor analyzed. Each was found to be an indicator of a single underlying political alienation construct, both in cross-sectional analysis and in over-time (replicated cross-sectional) analyses (Mason et al. 1985).

Still, these measures are subject to the same criticism as those from the other traditions. Because they deal with individual-level data, scarce phenomena and characteristics that hold true for only a small portion of the electorate may not be picked up by sampling, which includes only a fraction of the population. More critical, however, is the fact that phenomena that occur at the macro or "system" level may go undetected at the individual level. Finally, these measures, like the others discussed, are bound to a positivist image of the world, which does not consider the totality of social formation.[3]

Period Effects

The 1964 through 1980 CPS-NES presidential-year surveys have been pooled into one data set to better understand the fluctuations in political alienation from 1964 through 1980. To the degree that these fluctuations are due to secular, unspecifiable historical trends that affect all members of a population in a similar fashion, they can properly be labelled "period effects." In this study, period effects are variables that specify the year a respondent's interview was conducted. Thus, respondents are given codes of one for the year in which they were interviewed and a zero for all other years. These variables, therefore, provide a means of statistically controlling the effects of unexplained secular changes over time in the level of political alienation.

Sociodemographic Characteristics

Education is the number of years of formal schooling or the level of credentialing a person receives. Each respondent was dummy coded for either 0 to 8 years of education, 9 to 11 years of education, high-school education or the equivalent level of credentialing, 13 to 15 years of education, or the equivalent of a college education or more. Respondents were coded according to the number of years of academic training they received. In those cases where academic training was supplemented by vocational or the equivalent academic training, the respondent's level of education was increased only when that training provided a higher level of credentialing to the respondent; that is, only when some type of certification was received for participating in that training.

Income is the sum of money received by all members of the respondent's family prior to taxes, converted into constant 1980 dollars. Each respondent was assigned a score that corresponds to the midpoint of his or her income category. A Pareto curve estimate was used to derive midpoints for respondents whose incomes fell in the highest, open-ended income categories.

Next, the codes were converted into 1980 dollars by taking the national consumer price index (CPI) for the year in which the respondent's interview was conducted, dividing this CPI into the national CPI for 1980, and multiplying the dividend by the respondent's income category midpoint. Thus, the resulting income codes for different periods are relatively comparable for analysis purposes. In addition, respondents were categorized into income quintiles.

Race was divided between blacks and nonblacks. Respondents were coded one if they said their race was black and zero otherwise. Race was dichotomized for two major reasons: First, the political disaffection literature has usually examined black versus white (or more accurately nonblack) levels of political alienation. Such coding here, therefore, keeps the current research consistent with and comparable to earlier research in this tradition. Second, the examination of other nonwhite racial/ethnic groups becomes problematic because sample sizes for such groups are too small to carry out multivariate analysis.

Sex was divided between males and females. Respondents were coded one if they were male and zero otherwise.

Age is collapsed into six categories: younger than 30 years old, 30 to 39 years old, 40 to 49 years old, 50 to 59 years old, 60 to 69 years old, and 70 years or older. Respondents were dummy coded for the appropriate age categories.

Region of origin (i.e., region of socialization) was trichotomized. Respondents were dummy coded according to their region of socialization: the South, outside of the South but in the territorial United States and outside of the United States.

Political party identification (partisanship) was collapsed into three categories: Democrats, Republicans, and nonpartisans (those with no preference for Democrats or Republicans). Respondents who reported that they were Democrats or Independents with Democratic leanings were dummy coded as Democrats; Republicans and Independents with Republican leanings were coded as Republicans; and respondents with "third party" or no political party preferences were coded as nonpartisans.

The urbanicity of each respondent's city of residence was categorized as follows: one of the 12 largest Standard Metropolitan Statistical Areas (SMSA's), an SMSA other than one of the 12 largest, or an area that is not an SMSA. Respondents were dummy coded according to the urbanicity of their place of residence.

Marital status was initially categorized into four groups: single, married, divorced, widowed. These groups were then collapsed into two groups, married and unmarried. Respondents were assigned a score of one if they were currently married and currently living with their spouse (i.e., not separated), and zero otherwise.

Finally, region of current residence was collapsed into six categories: Northeast, Midwest, South, West, Mountain, and Border states. Respondents were dummy coded according to the region in which their current state of residence was located.

Now, this study moves on to examine the effects of these various variables on political alienation, and in doing so, it presents evidence relevant to the political personality, culture, and socialization theories discussed above.

A FIRST LOOK AT PATTERNS IN POLITICAL
ALIENATION

As mentioned previously, political personality, culture, and socialization explanations suggest that levels of alienation will vary by sociodemographic characteristics, and that levels and rates of alienation will
be virtually constant, net of compositional changes in the sociodemographic profile of the populace. Figure 1 presents results that pertain to
such formulations. This figure provides some evidence from the two
indicators of political alienation that lends support to one of the central
claims of personality, culture, and socialization theories.

In particular, the results show that both political inefficacy and political
distrust vary by such characteristics as educational attainment, income,
race, sex, and region. Generally, these sociodemographic differences are
more pronounced for the inefficacy dimension. For example, there is a
clear tendency for levels of political inefficacy to be higher among those
who have lower levels of education, lower incomes, are black, are female,
or live in the South. Lower levels of political inefficacy are associated
with those who have the opposing characteristics. These patterns are
not as clear cut for the distrust dimension; nevertheless, they still do
provide the potential for explaining drops and rises in political alienation
if the composition of the population has changed significantly over time.

One way to determine whether political alienation changed over time
(above and beyond fluctuations produced by demographic shifts) is by
using analysis strategies that control for the sociodemographic composition of the populace. Table 3 presents such an analysis. It shows the
mean levels of political inefficacy and political distrust by period from
1964 through 1980. These means are adjusted (statistically) for the effects
of the sociodemographic variables discussed earlier.

The results provide evidence that levels of inefficacy and distrust did
increase from 1964 through 1980, net of demographic variations. The
inefficacy index increased from an average score of 45.5 in 1964 to a
mean of 60.9 in 1980. Similarly, the distrust index climbed from 53.3 in
1964 to an average of 85.8 in 1980. These results are at odds with what
the political personality, culture, and socialization theory predicts. They
are, however, consistent with the predictions of the spirit of the times
theory. The particulars of this approach are presented below.

SPIRIT OF THE TIMES THEORIES

Spirit of the times explanations of fluctuations in political alienation
suggest that such trends reflect large-scale changes produced by specific
situations and historical events so pervasive that they affect virtually all
members of a society and lead them to respond in a similar fashion.
These explanations maintain, for example, that nearly all people in a

Figure 1
Levels of Political Alienation by Selected Sociodemographics

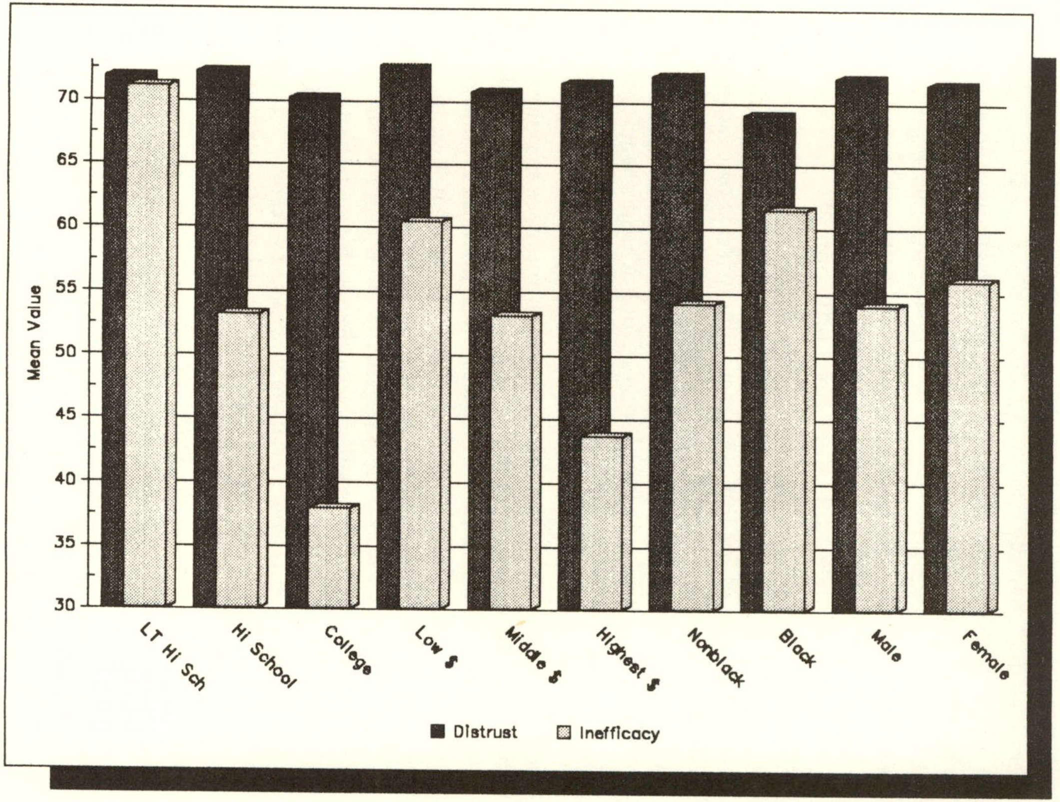

[handwritten: FOR vars in Fig 1, HOW not stated; no stats]

Table 3

Adjusted Mean Levels of Political Inefficacy and Distrust, 1964–80

	1964	1968	1972	1976	1980
Political Inefficacy	45.5	53.6	55.9	58.9	60.9
Political Distrust	53.3	63.2	71.7	82.1	85.8

Source: 1964-1980 American National Election Surveys

population will react similarly to wars, depressions, scandals, or other nationwide, politically-relevant events. They do not, however, suggest that the existence of pervasive, society-wide events will lead every group to have the same level or percentage distribution of political alienation. Differences between groups occur because groups have different starting points prior to the events of a period. But the general trend or pattern of fluctuations for all groups and classes will be similar for a given period.

Spirit of the times explanations usually present gross trends in political alienation and point to events of a period that supposedly cause those trends. Proponents of this perspective seldom take into account the possibility that patterns apparent for the total population may in fact contain significantly different subpopulation patterns. Generally, they do not rigorously examine underlying sociopolitical processes that may be in operation to create patterns of political alienation for a period. Nor do these explanations usually consider the possibility that common historical events may have differential effects on substantively different social groups and classes with different interests. Thus, proponents of this perspective do not ordinarily investigate the *net* differential effects of events on different classes in a systematic fashion. Instead, they posit that "trends in political alienation reflect historical period effects affecting all members of the population in a similar fashion" (Cutler and Bengtson 1976, p. 47).

[handwritten margin note: no ref to mann here; should there be?]

In their analysis of political alienation, House and Mason (1975) maintained that the trends during the period from 1952 through 1968 reflected aggregate period-effect changes in the population as a whole. They argued that such trends did not represent simple aggregations of changes in the levels or rates of political alienation in any identifiable race, sex, region, education, or income group. At first glance, these findings appear to support the general malaise, "spirit of the times" position in that they suggest no single clear-cut explanation of the trends in political alienation; however, House and Mason's explanation of these trends differed markedly from the spirit of the times explanation inasmuch as they specified a mechanism by which political alienation changed uniformly (from 1952 through 1968) throughout the various subpopulations, but was not changing for the same reasons across these subpopulations. In other words, they agreed with the notion that changes in political alienation were uniform, as predicted by the spirit of the times explanation, but they did not agree with that perspective's reasons for the uniformity.

Generally, the spirit of the times theory is a largely post hoc, residual explanatory scheme in several respects. First, it says little about the nature and sources of cross-sectional variation in alienation. It takes these as givens and deals only with changes over time from a cross-sectional baseline. Second, it fails to articulate with general theories of political alienation. Rather it is a special theory for dealing with marked historical variations that did not seem to fit well with existing theories. Third, it is a fall-back explanation in that analysts use it essentially to explain variation that is unexplainable in other terms, and it offers no clear basis for predicting future historical change. Thus, it is difficult to confirm or reject, but remains practicable as long as no one advances a more specific and predictive theory to account for observed historical variations in alienation.

Perhaps the most prominent recent version of spirit of the times theory comes from S. M. Lipset and William Schneider (1983). In their book, *Confidence Gap*, they demonstrate that declines in confidence occurred not only for the political institutions, but also for such American institutions as business, education, organized labor, the military, and religion. They argue that America experienced "a widespread loss of faith in the leadership of business, government, labor, and other private and public institutions at more or less the same time" (p. 3). To account for these patterns, they correctly point to the occurrence of such real-life events as the civil rights movement, the Vietnam War, and Watergate. They fail to acknowledge, however, that these real-life events had differential effects on the levels of alienation for different groups in the society. For example, blacks and whites did not respond in the same way to the civil rights movement. From the early 1960s through the mid-1970s, while an overwhelming majority of whites consistently reported that "civil rights leaders [were] trying to push too fast," less than 10 percent of blacks held such views. "Hawks" and "doves" had different opinions of and preferences for actions by the government during the Vietnam War. For example, Arthur Miller (1974) reports that between 1964 and 1970, political trust declined much more sharply among those who favored an immediate withdrawal from Vietnam than among those who favored the policies practiced by the Johnson and Nixon administrations. They responded differently to the policies pursued and to the ultimate outcome of the war. Similarly, not all groups' levels of alienation increased to the same extent with the resignation of Richard Nixon during the Watergate scandal. Between 1972 and 1976, Republicans' levels of trust in the political institutions declined at a rate that was more than 40 percent greater than that for Democrats.

In pushing the idea that real events were the source of political alienation, Lipset and Schneider are not incorrect. They are just incomplete. Unlike many in the political personality, culture, and socialization camp, they show that patterns in trust and confidence reflect some objective realities. For them, therefore, levels of political alienation are not just figments of people's realities. Levels of confidence do correspond to real events that would give people more (or less) reason to trust that policymakers are exploring policies that are consonant with their particular interest (and, therefore, worthy of trust). For this reason, Lipset and Schneider are able to track, with a great deal of success, the fluctuations in levels of trust and confidence in the political institutions.

While Lipset and Schneider's pragmatic approach does a good job of explaining the overall patterns that occurred in the past, there are, nevertheless, some limitations in their approach. Like others who use the spirit of the times approach, they do not specify sufficient conditions for differential levels and rates of change. They fail to examine closely the role of the state in augmenting the efforts of various factions involved in struggles over policies. Thus, their theoretical perspective prevents them from realizing that middle-American disenchantment with the operation and results of capitalism spilled over to such capitalist institutions as government, business, organized (some would say bourgeois) labor unions, profit-oriented religious organizations, and the expansionist military. As movement activists of the 1960s and 1970s undermined the hegemony of capitalism, the authority of all of these institutions was called into question in varying degrees. Changes in the levels of disenchantment with these institutions among the citizenry were not necessarily uniform across sociodemographic and political groups, however.

Because spirit of the times explanations claim that common events have similar effects on the total population, they predict that changes in the level and rate of political alienation are uniform for virtually all groups in society. Thus, this perspective leads one to expect that changes in political alienation should be similar for the wealthy and the poor, workers and owners, and the middle layers and others. The spirit of the times theory, then, essentially posits that there are substantial rises (and falls) in political alienation over time that occur uniformly across class boundaries and are not explainable by sociodemographic (compositional) change. Such changes will reflect significant historical events that are themselves hard to predict.

Much of the prior research on trends in political alienation has been consistent with spirit of the times explanations. Major increases in political alienation during the 1960s and 1970s appeared to be uniform

[handwritten: again no detail on stats, and no way to tell SIZE of differences nor to SG.]

across virtually all sociodemographic subgroups of the population (e.g., House and Mason 1975).

Figure 2, however, presents a very different picture of the changes in political alienation. It shows that there were substantial variations across classes, as capitalists, the middle layers, traditional workers, and the poor differed in the reasons for changes in the levels of their political alienation.

For each class and class fraction, this figure presents the percentage change in average levels of political alienation. Note that the averages for each class and class fraction are adjusted means based on a regression analysis that has controlled for the effects of such factors as gender, race, region of current residence, region of origin, age, education, income, urbanicity, and political party affiliation; thus, all results reported are *net* of these sociodemographic (compositional) effects.

These results are directly contrary to political culture and socialization theory expectations that levels of political alienation would remain constant net of compositional changes in the population. Indeed, Americans from all classes increasingly believed that they lacked meaningful input into government decision making. The mean level of political alienation increased by more than 20 percent from 1964 to 1980. Since these changes in political alienation were not uniform across class boundaries, they also undermine the predictions of the spirit of the times formulation. For example, Figure 2 shows that from 1964 to 1968, the capitalist class experienced substantially larger increases in their levels of political inefficacy than all other classes. In contrast, from 1968 to 1972 when capitalists were experiencing decreases in their levels of inefficacy, the middle layers experienced increases. From 1972 to 1976, when the traditional working class remained constant in their levels of alienation, the middle layers, the poor, and capitalists experienced increases. In addition, from 1976 to 1980, the middle layers were the only class fractions to experience nontrivial rises in levels of political inefficacy. These findings are contrary to the forecasts of spirit of the times formulators. They are, however, consistent with a third political disaffection perspective: political structure and interest group theories.

POLITICAL STRUCTURE AND INTEREST GROUP THEORIES

Political structure and interest group theories share with the spirit of the times approach the notion that large-scale changes and specific situations and historical events produce political orientations. They share with the political personality, culture, and socialization approach the idea that political orientations differ by sociodemographic characteristics. Yet, these theories differ from both the spirit of the times perspective

Figure 2
Percent Change in Political Inefficacy by Class, 1964–80

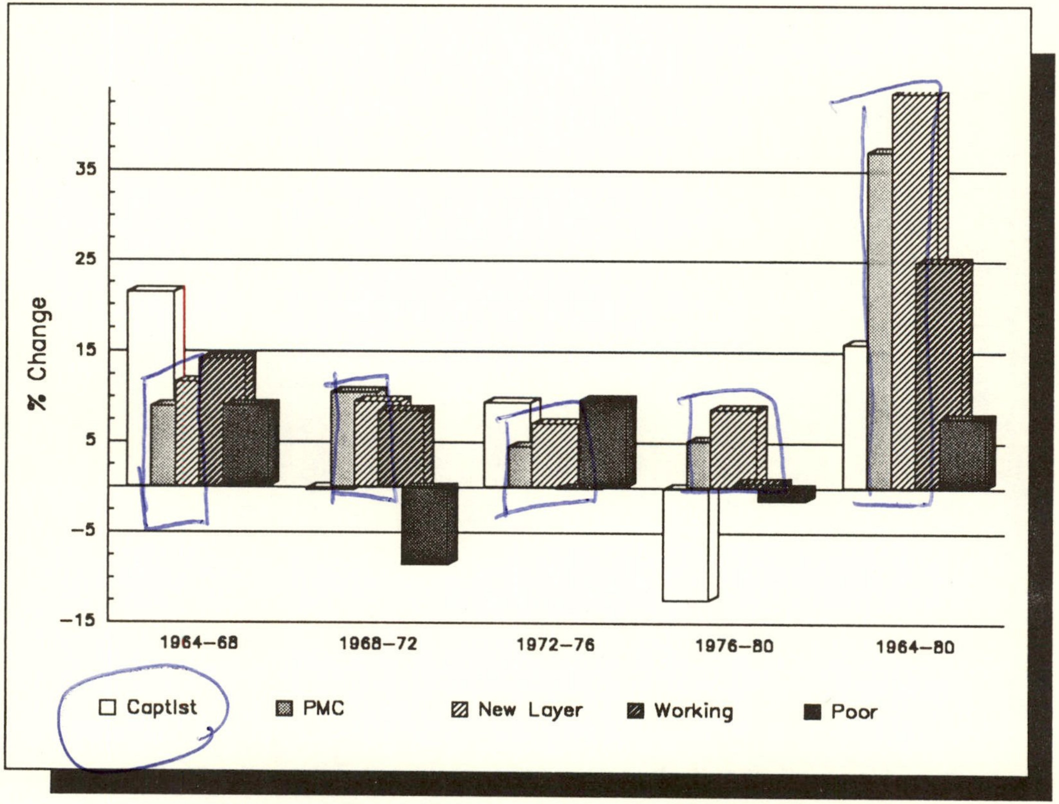

and the political culture and socialization approach in some fundamental ways. Specifically, unlike the spirit of the times framework, the political interest group approach maintains that large-scale changes and historical events are generally divisive. Such events, therefore, produce differential reactions and orientations among the population. Unlike those works that use sociodemographic characteristics as surrogates for political culture, the political interest group framework does not see political attitudes and orientations as long-enduring nor as necessarily supportive of the prevailing political culture. Rather, this framework sees political orientations as dynamic and ever-changing in response to politically relevant issues.

Political interest group theorists suggest that political orientations in general—and political trust and efficacy in particular—grow out of political interests (e.g., Gamson 1968a; House and Mason 1975; Miller 1983; Miller et al. 1976; Easton 1965; Guest 1974; Hibbs et al. 1982; Iyengar 1980; and Markus 1979). They imply that political issues and events will become salient to people to the degree that they affect perceived political interests. Moreover, when political issues, events, decisions, or policies further their interests, people are more likely to view their political institutions and policymakers as trustworthy. They will feel efficacious to the extent that they are able to influence the direction of policies and events. In short, actors feel less politically alienated under such circumstances. Conversely, when policies and events go against their political interests, such actors are more likely to feel politically alienated.

There are some reasons why individuals may not feel politically alienated even when the interests of their group are not furthered by political events and policy decisions. First, there is the issue of "cross-cutting cleavages" and "cross-cutting solidarities," which points to the fact that each individual has simultaneous identification and affiliation with several primary groups, social aggregates, complex organizations, religious groups, social classes, etc. With such competing memberships, it is difficult to determine *a priori* which will serve as appropriate reference groups for a given political decision. Secondly, and along the same lines, people may belong to groups that are so amorphous and disorganized that they do not feel as if their fates depend on the fates of their groups. Thirdly, people may agree with the rules by which decisions are made to such an extent that they are willing to accept virtually all political outcomes as just, regardless of their effects, as long as they conform to the proper decision-making process.

Proponents of this framework posit, at least implicitly, that political interests usually crystallize around identifiable sociodemographic characteristics. Interests determine political orientations. Political orientations, in turn, can be linked to identifiable groups involved in "zero-sum" competitions for political outcomes in which there are necessarily losers and winners. When an interest group favoring a particular out-come has its interests furthered, opposing groups have their interests set back by the same amount. For example, when the rich win, the poor lose. Similarly, to the degree that workers win, owners lose. This does not mean, however, that the issues and events at hand will be of equal salience to all groups affected. Nor does it mean that all groups involved will be immediately identifiable as having vested interests in an outcome. Nevertheless, with any given political decision, to the degree that there is the perception that there are real and nontrivial interests at stake, there is the chance that some groups will experience increases in their levels of political alienation and other groups (with opposing interests) will experience decreases in their alienation.

So, this approach is relatively straightforward in predicting which groups will feel politically alienated: Those groups that believe their interests are not being served. However, because of the several quali-fications presented by its proponents, it is not very easy to determine which individuals of those groups will feel politically alienated. It is clear, though, that this framework predicts differential rates of change in the level and incidence of political alienation unless, as House and Mason (1975) pointed out, different issues alienate all groups to the same degree within the same period. Nevertheless, whether people trust gov-ernment at any given time depends primarily on how well it is respond-ing to their needs and interests at that time. Similarly, how efficacious they feel at any time is primarily a function of how able they feel to influence the government at that time. Their history of previous efficacy, politically and otherwise, is likely to be important, however. Political trust and (to a somewhat lesser degree) political efficacy are likely to vary over time and across groups at a given point in time because chang-ing policies and events are generally assumed to be differentially favor-able to the interests and needs of different groups. Thus, this theory expects changes in political alienation during periods of sharp change in political events and policies. Some groups' levels increase while those of others decrease, and some groups' levels change more rapidly than those of others.

Figure 3 presents results for the political distrust index, which taps perceptions of government trustworthiness. Just as was the case for the inefficacy index, the results contradict both the spirit of the times ex-planation and political personality, culture, and socialization theory. Also, similar to previous findings are results that are consistent with and supportive of political structure and interest group theories. In-creases in political distrust were substantial (more than a 50% increase from 1964 to 1980) and class-differentiated.

There were dramatic increases in political distrust for each class. The extent of increase in political distrust among the middle layers, for

Figure 3
Percent Change in Political Distrust by Class, 1964–80

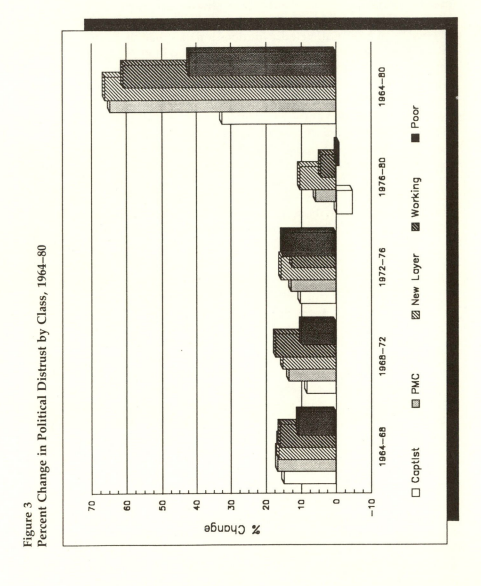

no agua for inefficacy!

What are the UNITS here. are the diffs sig?

Figure 4
Changes in Political Distrust for the PMC and New Layer, 1964–80

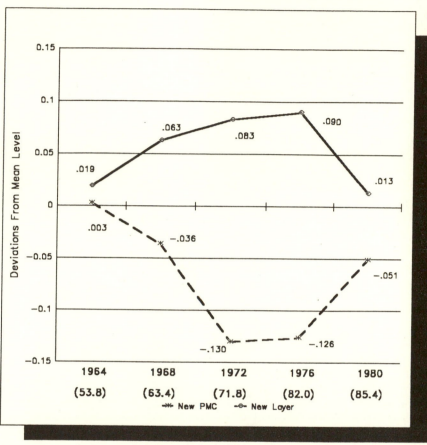

example, was more dramatic than for other classes, especially after 1968 when these class fractions always had higher-than-average increases in political distrust.

Figure 4 shows that there were also some differences in the patterns of change among members of the middle layers. In particular, during the 1970s, members of the new layer had larger relative increases in their levels of political distrust than their PMC counterparts. Between 1964 and 1976, when the new layer's net rate of increase outpaced the average, the PMC's net rate of increase actually declined relative to those of other class fractions. These net differences in rates of change, while not large, are at least suggestive of distinctions between these class fractions.

Given these findings, it is evident that changes in political alienation did not come from compositional changes in the population. It is also clear that these trends in alienation did not reflect only those large-scale historical events that affected all members of the society in a similar fashion. Rather, these findings suggest that changes in political alienation were class-differentiated and reflective of issues and events that were divisive and salient to different segments of the populace. In short, these findings suggest that in order to achieve a better understanding of the nature and sources of class-based changes in political alienation, it will be necessary to focus more attention on the role of the state and the impact that government policies and decisions had on particular classes and class fractions. It will also be important to examine the role that these policies and decisions played in generating perceptions of the political system for different classes. This will require examining not only those alienating policies and events that cut across class boundaries, but also those policies and events that brought about dramatic changes *within* classes over time.

The next chapter discusses the role of the state itself in the generation of political alienation through its actions and policies. It also discusses why different classes and class fractions have vastly different predispositions toward the state and its actions.

NOTES

1. Statistics are based on pairwise deletions of missing data; that is, correlations are based on different subsets of the data set, depending on the missing data for the variables under consideration. The maximum N is 10,074; the effective N (i.e., used to generate correlation matrices) is 7,795.

2. The examination of the effects of specific issue-attitudes on political alienation is beyond the scope of this study; thus, issue-attitude effects are not explicitly tested here. The inclusion of period effects does, however, capture some of these effects.

3. As Marcuse (1964, p. 170) points out, much of social science remains at the level of the "facticity of the given." The difference between reality as it presently appears and its essential qualities is not distinguished. He argues that such analyses have the effect of justifying the status quo whether they intend to or not.

This chapter is critical to his argument and does not make its case!

Chapter Five

Squeezing the Middle: Alienated Politics and the Welfare Split

There is fairly widespread consensus that there have been quite massive shifts in public attitudes toward the political institutions. *Why* such changes have occurred, however, remains a debatable issue. Indeed, as pointed out earlier, a number of formulations have been developed to explain why some Americans believe their government, political leaders, policymakers, and political institutions are unresponsive and untrustworthy. In addition to the political disaffection perspectives discussed in Chapter 4, there are a number of explanations that pay more attention to the role of the state itself in the generation of political alienation. Neo-Marxian theories, in particular, commonly maintain that Western capitalist states will experience crises of legitimacy because they are caught up in the contradictory objectives of maintaining conditions of profitable capital accumulation for capitalists at the same time that they try to ensure the continued legitimacy of a fundamentally exploitative system.

There are, however, reasons to question this line of reasoning. For example, it is quite possible for a society to secure the allegiance of its citizenry "without any assurance that the resulting policy, action, or societal structure will not be alienating" (Etzioni 1961). This can happen because differences in power lead to inauthentic consensus in support of patterns that are not responsive to the needs of the weak. In other words, it is quite possible that conditions of "objective" political alienation will not automatically translate into feelings that the state's actions are illegitimate. Nevertheless, the general consensus among neo-Marxian theories is that fluctuations in feelings of political alienation among the general population correspond to the state's efforts to support profit-making for the capitalist class and corporations.

The primary purpose of this chapter is to use insights from the neo-Marxian literature, which investigates the crisis tendencies of the capitalist state to inform the empirically oriented literature on political alienation. In addition, it seeks to broaden neo-Marxian formulations so that they can account for the drastic increases in the levels of political alienation that have occurred in the United States over the past 20 years.

ALIENATED POLITICS THEORIES

Though there are differences among the alienated politics theories, there are some central premises, arguments, and themes common to most of them. For example, most of them are neo-Marxian in orientation, and thus they see political alienation as a consequence of the operations of the capitalist state under liberal democracy. More specifically, most versions of alienated politics theories start with the premise that, in contemporary capitalist societies, the state serves two mutually contradictory functions: accumulation and legitimacy. In other words, at the same time that the state promotes actions and conditions that will facilitate capital accumulation for owners of the means of production, it must maintain the myth that its actions are in the interests of "the people" from whom it derives its power. It is this fundamental contradiction between the state's role in the capital accumulation process and its need to have the support (or at least the inactivity) of its objectively alienated citizenry that is postulated to be the driving force toward a legitimacy crisis of the state.

James O'Connor (1973; 1984), for example, argues that because of the inability of private capital to ensure conditions that facilitate the realizations of profit, the capitalist state involves itself in producing such conditions. But when the state is too heavily involved in subsidizing capital and fulfilling its accumulation function, the contradictions between accumulation and legitimation may become manifest, especially among those who do not share in the benefits of the state's involvement. In fact, under such conditions, disgruntled working-class and poor people, who can disrupt the functioning of the state and the accumulation process, provide an ever-present threat to state managers. Because of the existence of this segment of the society, which bears the brunt of the functioning of the capitalist economic system, the state seeks to demonstrate that it is morally legitimate by showing itself to be humane and representative of all of the people. It attempts to legitimate its accumulation policies, the capitalist relations of production, and the electoral process by making symbolic concessions to the economically disenfranchized. These concessions often take the form of capital outlays for social welfare and safety net programs. Thus, the state deals with the political challenge posed by these segments of society by enhancing their "social wages" and subsidizing them economically through social welfare programs. However, repression is also an option that can be used when such subsidies interfere with the accumulation process.

O'Connor goes on to argue that, on most occasions, the delicate balance between accumulation and legitimation is maintained, and the contradictions resulting from the pursuit of these two mutually contradictory objectives are concealed. Under conditions of economic and accumulation crises, however, these contradictions become manifest. For example, during economic recessions, it becomes necessary for the state to become directly involved in facilitating accumulation by providing capital outlays to industry. During such times, the state will need more revenue to finance such subsidies as speculative building, the granting of free land to industry, research and development used by industry, state-supported training of industrial workers, etc.

Also during recessions, inasmuch as "relief policies are designed to mute civil disorder . . . " (Piven and Cloward 1971, p. xiii), the need for money for legitimating functions becomes greater. However, as O'Connor (1973, p. 151) points out, "decelerating economic growth forces cutbacks in outlays on the surplus population." This is true because more money for legitimation means less money for accumulation and vice versa. So, in order to be able to subsidize capital more, the state needs either to increase its revenues or decrease its other expenditures, or else a "structural gap"—a fiscal crisis in which state expenditures increase much more rapidly than the means of financing them—will result.

To do away with this structural gap, again, the state must either increase its revenues or decrease its expenditures. To increase its revenues, the state basically must raise taxes. This is an unacceptable solution to elected representatives who must deliver lower levels of taxation in order to get re-elected and who must give corporations everlarger tax write-offs in order to leave business with higher levels of profit after taxes. Reliance on increased taxation, moreover, sets off such occurrences as tax revolts, calls for cuts in government spending, and demands for balanced budgets at the same time that there are demands on the state for more costly social programs and more subsidies to private industry. Thus, in the long run this alternative is no real solution to the accumulation-legitimacy contradiction because the populace becomes increasingly unwilling to have their taxes raised in order to subsidize private industry.

Another solution to the accumulation-legitimacy contradiction is for the state to reduce its expenditures. To decrease expenditures, the state can reduce spending for social welfare programs; however, this solution is unacceptable because social welfare programs are a primary source of legitimacy for the state, especially among those who must bear the brunt of the economic woes of capitalism. It is unlikely that the state could afford to cut spending to the "necessary" levels during recessions because this is precisely when such spending is most necessary to prevent social protest and unrest. Also, some programs such as social security and education have taken on the nature of "sacred cows" in which they are considered rights and, therefore, cannot be dismantled without serious repercussions (in terms of voting out of office those elected officials who vote for such cuts).

There are some other short-term, stop-gap measures that the state can take to alleviate the accumulation-legitimacy contradiction. One such measure would have private industry become more directly involved in the provision of social services to those who might otherwise challenge the state's legitimacy. This would only be a stop-gap solution because ultimately,

[T]he accumulation of social capital [would occur] within a political framework, [and] there [would be] a great deal of waste, duplication, and overlapping of state projects and services. Some claims [would] conflict and cancel one another out. . . . [There would be] struggles around the control of the budget . . . [which would] impair the fiscal capacity of the system to produce surplus (O'Connor 1973, p. 10).

Moreover, as the state becomes more directly and overtly a facilitator of the accumulation of surplus for private industry, the accumulation process becomes more politicized, and the distinctions between "laissez-faire" capitalism and state socialism for capitalists and corporations becomes less clear. As this distinction blurs, the state loses its legitimacy as an agent of the people, and its actions are called into question by groups mobilized against the demystified actions and policies of the state.

A fourth solution to the accumulation-legitimacy contradiction is for the liberal democratic state to undergo a major transformation. The state can either choose legitimacy to the neglect of accumulation, or it can choose accumulation to the negation of legitimacy. In the former, the state takes on the character of a socialist democracy; in the latter case, it opts for repressive fascism. In either case, however, the legitimacy crisis is "solved" because the accumulation-legitimacy contradiction is virtually done away with.

AN ALTERNATIVE, "WELFARE SPLIT" MODEL

Alienated politics formulations call attention to a number of factors that are absent from political disaffection explanations of changes in political alienation. Although these explanations are not inconsistent with the idea that changes in levels of political alienation were not uniform for the various classes and class layers, *as formulated*, they do not offer a great deal of promise in accounting for the dramatic increases in political alienation that occurred among the middle layers.

In particular, these formulations argue that there is an inherent contradiction between the state's efforts to facilitate profits for the capitalist class and its attempts to secure the support of noncapitalists. It is also clear from such discussions that they would suggest that fluctuations in political distrust reflect efforts on the part of the capitalist state to facilitate profit-making for corporations and the capitalist class, as well as the ability of these corporations and capitalists to realize profits. More specifically, these theories would lead one to expect that levels of political alienation generally increase as state subsidies to corporations and levels of corporate profits increase. Moreover, they would lead one to believe that the most dramatic increases in political alienation during the past two decades should have occurred among the poor and working class. In short, they suggest that there is an "accumulation-legitimacy contradiction," which prevents the capitalist state from receiving widespread citizen support while it is engaged in practices that enhance the economic position of the capitalist class.

In contrast, the argument here is that economic expansion and growth—another way of talking about capital accumulation—provide a justification for the capitalist class's having greater advantages than other layers of the population. Accumulation and legitimacy—that is, economic expansion and support for the political institutions of the state—need not be viewed as mutually exclusive of each other. Indeed, the opposite case can be made: When the economy is contracting, economic misery is widespread, and disaccumulation is taking place, the basis for advantages among capitalists is undermined and the state becomes the target of discontent because state managers—not corporate actors nor the capitalist class—are held responsible for the performance of the economy. Worsening economic conditions erode the legitimacy of the state, not so much because they worsen the conditions of the powerless (who already experience high levels of misery), but rather because they undermine the bases of advantages for the capitalist class. With continual growth, the capitalist class continues to present the justification that everyone gains. During periods of economic stagnation and recession, however, this class can accumulate wealth only by extracting additional surplus from those who are not ordinarily superexploited. Thus, subsidies to industry, economic expansions, and subsequent increases in capital accumulation should *increase* rather than decrease trust in the political institutions of the state.

The argument proposed here is that capital accumulation in itself is *not* the source of distrust toward the state. Rather, distrust occurs when the state attempts to facilitate capital accumulation at the expense of those in the middle layers who do not ordinarily experience the actions of the state as harmful to their interests. Such attempts to facilitate accumulation at the expense of the middle layers will occur during periods of "stagflation" and will result in the reduction of the social wage and the curtailment of social programs that benefit the middle layers. In other words, the relationships between political alienation and accumulation and between political alienation and welfare spending are conditional: Increasing levels of capital accumulation generally lead to trust in the political institutions; increasing levels of spending for social welfare generally do not lead to trust in the state. But the elimination of social welfare programs, especially when economic misery is high and the economy is contracting, increases political alienation among the new layer and the poor.

Because groups with low structural locations (e.g., the poor) generally lack routine access to policymakers and state managers, state policies usually go against their interests and have deleterious effects on them; thus, they feel politically alienated. As recessions deepen and economic conditions worsen, however, the new layer's rates of misery increase much more rapidly, and they join the ranks of the alienated at a much faster rate.

In her study of those who where unemployed in the 1960s and 1970s, Leventman (1981, pp. xv–xvi) points out that:

Expanding economic horizons in the sixties were eclipsed in the leaner seventies. . . . All areas of the economy, all types of industry, and all levels of the occupational hierarchy were affected. . . . For the first time, unemployment cut across occupational prestige hierarchies. . . . Recent college graduates, state and municipal employees, engineers and scientists, teachers and academics, librarians and psychologists, even young lawyers and middle-aged business executives acutely felt the labor market squeeze. . . .

She goes on to argue that "[p]rofessionals unemployed in the seventies felt a particular sense of betrayal by a society that had allowed them success and esteem as the price of their faith in the system."

In short, during the 1970s, growing proportions of the new layer experienced high levels of economic misery, and those experiences translated into increasingly negative assessments of the political institutions.

These dramatic increases in levels of economic misery, as well as state policies that relegated greater proportions of the middle layers to those higher levels of economic misery, were among the driving forces behind the dramatic declines in trust in American political system. This is not to say that economic misery per se accounts for changes in assessments of the state; rather, changes in the levels of economic misery triggered changes in other macroeconomic factors, which in turn influenced perceptions of the state's trustworthiness.

Of course, several other factors had effects on political alienation. In particular, previous chapters demonstrated that several sociodemographic variables affect levels of political alienation: income levels, education, race, gender, etc. Generally, though, groups that experienced the fastest rates of increase in economic misery also experienced the most dramatic increases in political alienation. During the mid–1960s through the late 1970s such groups included those with middle structural locations: the new layer and the professional-managerial class.

State policies that determined levels of industrial subsidy, levels of state indebtedness, and levels of spending for social welfare also affected trust in the government. Many of these effects were indirect and conditional. In particular, spending for social welfare programs had a conditional relationship to political alienation. That is, spending for social welfare increased trust in the government among those who benefited from such programs, but generally decreased trust otherwise. Similarly, state subsidies to industry facilitated capital accumulation, and thus, they indirectly increased trust in the political institutions. Meanwhile, such subsidies increased deficits in state budgets, which in turn reduced trust in the political institutions of the state. Fiscal gaps, that is, state budget deficits, also had both direct and indirect negative effects on trust in the government. Because such deficits generally decreased economic growth (capital accumulation), they facilitated assessments that the state was untrustworthy. Moreover, these fiscal gaps also produced distrust toward the state in their own right. Consistent with earlier arguments about expansion of the economy being a central basis for trust in the government, capital accumulation, net of all other factors, is hypothesized to increase trust in the political institutions of the state.

To summarize the predictions of the welfare split framework, a conceptual diagram is presented in Figure 5. This conceptual model, for example, suggests that the level of misery in the society has both direct and indirect effects on political alienation. The model posits that, as economic conditions worsen and the level of misery in the society increases, distrust in the political institutions increases, subsidies to private industry increase, and the level of welfare spending increases. Subsidies to industry also have direct and indirect effects on political distrust. As subsidies to industry increase, assessments that the state's political institutions are not trustworthy decrease. Also, as the level of subsidy to industry increases, political distrust decreases, the level of welfare spending decreases and the level of accumulation decreases. As welfare spending increases, distrust in the state's political institutions increases among those who do not directly benefit from welfare expenditures, but

Figure 5
Conceptual Diagram of the Welfare Split Model

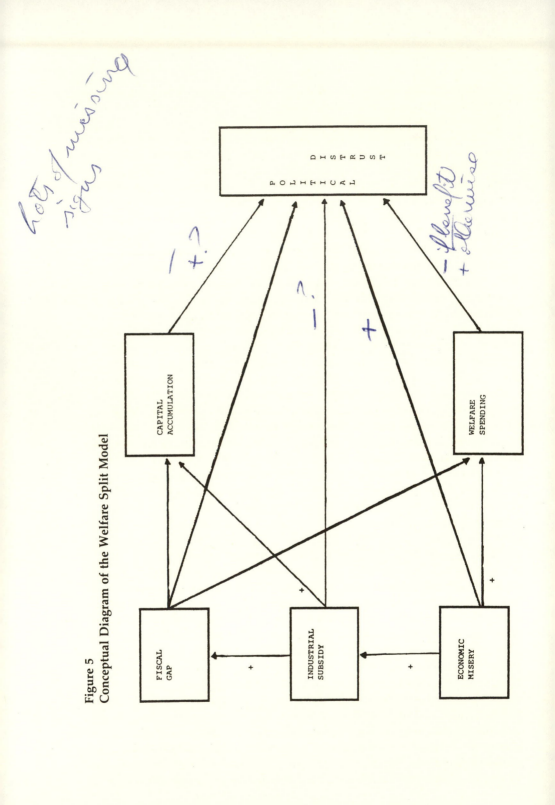

decreases among those who do gain from such spending. Finally, as the economy expands and capital accumulation by corporations increases, political distrust increases.

The alienated politics model and the alternative welfare split model make discrepant predictions about the nature of political alienation and the nature of changes in political alienation over time. For example, the alienated politics explanation leads one to expect that increases in capital accumulation lead to lower levels of trust in the political institutions of the state; the alternative explanation predicts that capital accumulation (i.e., economic expansion) leads to higher levels of trust in the political institutions. Similarly, the alienated politics model predicts that the facilitation of capital accumulation has negative effects on the levels of trust in the government; the alternative explanation claims that industrial subsidies, a means of facilitating capital accumulation, lead to higher levels of trust in government inasmuch as they facilitate economic expansion. These explanations also make different predictions about the effects of social welfare spending on levels of political alienation: The alienated politics perspective predicts that such spending will have positive effects on levels of trust in government; the alternative perspective predicts that welfare spending will generally decrease trust in government except among those who benefit from such spending. These competing perspectives do concur on some points, however. For example, both predict that increases in state indebtedness and economic misery lead to higher levels of political distrust.

To determine what role state policies played in generating class-based changes in political alienation, data that reflect the nature of changes in these policies and political distrust are presented below. But first, a brief discussion of the data and data sources is presented.

DEFINITIONS AND OPERATIONALIZATIONS

The data used to test the formulations discussed above come from the Center for Political Studies' National Election Study's 1964–80 presidential-election-year surveys (N = 10,074), the U.S. Department of Commerce, *Handbook of Labor Statistics*, and *Industrial Development* (1964–80). For all macro-level variables, respondents were assigned values that corresponded to the values for their current states of residence. These data were used to operationalize such concepts as capital accumulation, welfare spending, structural gap, subsidies to industry, and economic misery.

Political Alienation. Because the focus here is on changes in levels of trust in the American political system, the central dimension of political alienation of concern is political trust. Accordingly, the political distrust measure (described in Chapter 4) will be of central concern.

Capital Accumulation. Capital accumulation is "the reproduction of capitalistic social relations on an ever-expanding scale through the conver-
sion of surplus value into new constant and variable capital" (E. O.
Wright 1979, p. 113). It is the process by which wealth is generated. On
an ongoing basis, it involves guaranteeing that revenues—increases in
owners' claims to probable future economic benefits—increase more rapidly than expenditures. In other words, accumulation takes place when
owners receive incomes that are greater than their losses for a given
period of time.

Accumulation is operationalized as follows: The net, after-tax incomes
of corporations and proprietors were determined for each presidential
election year from 1964 through 1980 by using data from the U.S. Department of Commerce. The incomes for each year were then standard-
ized into constant 1980 dollars by using the implicit gross national
products deflator for each year. The natural logarithms of these constant
dollars were then calculated.

Misery/Worsening Economic Conditions. Misery refers to a state of suf-
fering and want resulting from public policies that have deleterious
effects on identifiable groups. Worsening economic conditions exist
when the level or incidence of misery increases from time$_1$ to time$_2$.
Misery was operationalized as the sum of race-by-gender group-specific
unemployment rates plus the annual rate of inflation for each presidential election year from 1964 through 1980. Worsening economic conditions are changes in level of misery from 1964 through 1980.

Welfare Spending. Welfare spending is the amount of money in constant
1980 dollars that each state spent on social welfare programs per capita.

Subsidies to Industry. Subsidies to industry refer to all gifts of public
money, goods, services, or property to private enterprise. Subsidies that
states made available to industry include: (1) state-financed speculative
building; (2) free land for industry; (3) state funds for private recreational
projects; (4) state programs to promote research and development or
university research and development facilities made available to industry; (5) state incentives to industry to train unemployed workers; (6)
corporate income tax exemptions; (7) tax exemptions to industry for land
capital or equipment improvements; (8) tax exemptions on the value of
inventoried goods; (9) business tax credits for the use of specified state
products; (10) accelerated depreciation of industrial equipment; (11)
state-sponsored industrial development commission or authority; (12)
revenue bond financing; (13) state loans for building construction; (14)
state loans for equipment and machinery; and (15) incentives for establishing plants in areas of high unemployment.

Structural/Fiscal Gap. The structural gap refers to a fiscal crisis in which
there is an inherent tendency for state expenditures to increase faster

than the means of financing them. This variable is operationalized as the per capita state debt (in constant 1980 dollars) for each state.

why by state? why not federal?

Sociodemographic Characteristics

Education is the number of years of formal schooling or the level of credentialing a person receives. Respondents were coded for the number of years of academic training they received. In those cases where academic training was supplemented by vocational or other nonacademic training, the respondent's level of education was increased when that additional training provided a higher level of credentialing to the respondent; that is only when some type of certification was received for participation in that training.

Income is the sum of money received by all members of the respondent's family prior to taxes, converted into constant 1980 dollars. Each respondent was assigned a score that corresponded to the midpoint of his income category. (A Pareto curve estimate was used to derive midpoints for respondents whose incomes fell in the highest, open-ended income categories.) Next, the codes were converted into 1980 dollars by taking the national consumer price index (CPI) for the year in which the respondent's interview was conducted, dividing this CPI into the national CPI for 1980, and multiplying the dividend by the respondent's income category midpoint. Thus, the resulting income codes for different periods were comparable for analysis purposes.

Race was divided between blacks and nonblacks. Respondents were coded one if they said their race was black and zero otherwise.

Gender was divided between males and females. Respondents were coded one if they were male and zero otherwise.

Political party identification (partisanship) was divided into three categories: Democrats, Republicans, and nonpartisans. Respondents who reported that they were Democrats or Independents with Democratic leanings were coded as Democrats; Republicans and Independents with Republican leanings were coded as Republicans; and respondents with "third party," Independent, or no political party preferences were coded as nonpartisans.

Class position is defined and measured as described previously (in Chapter 1).

A LOOK AT SOME MORE RESULTS

In order to assess the claims of the alienated politics approach versus those of the alternative welfare split perspective, a fully recursive path model that corresponds to the conceptual model in Figure 5 was spec-

ified. Path analysis is a data-analytic technique that enables one to measure the direct and indirect effects of the variables on each other. In
addition, it allows one to examine the causal processes underlying the
observed relationships. Finally, path analysis allows one to determine
the relative importance of alternative paths of influence.

Figure 6 presents head-to-head tests of the competing predictions of
the alienated politics model and the alternative model in a path-analytic
format. The diagram presents the simultaneous effects of capital accumulation, welfare spending, state indebtedness, industrial subsidies,
and economic misery on levels of distrust in America's political institutions. In addition, the direct and indirect effects of these factors on
political alienation are presented as path coefficients (beta weights),
which illustrate the strength and direction of the relationship between
the variables of interest. For each exogenous (dependent) variable, the
percentage of its variance explained by its predictors is presented in the
box that corresponds to that variable.

For the most part, the results in Figure 6 are counter to what the
alienated politics model predicts. At the same time, they are far more
consistent with, though not fully supportive of, the alternative welfare
split model. More specifically, capital accumulation decreases levels of
political alienation. This finding is in the opposite direction of what the
alienated politics explanation predicts, but is supportive of the alternative perspective (at $p<.05$). The relationship between welfare spending and political alienation is also counter to the expectations of the
alienated politics model and supportive of the welfare split perspective:
Welfare spending significantly increases political distrust (at $p<.01$).

Other factors in Figure 6 are also in the direction predicted by the
split model, though not all of these factors attain statistical significance.
For example, as predicted by both the alienated politics model and the
alternative model, state indebtedness increases political distrust. This
relationship does not attain statistical significance, however. The relationship between economic misery and political alienation does attain
statistical significance (at $p<.01$). As predicted by both explanations,
political distrust increases as economic misery increases. The relationship between industrial subsidies and political alienation also attains
statistical significance (at $p<.01$). As subsidies increase, political alienation decreases. This finding is contrary to the expectations of the alienated politics theory, but it supports the claims of the alternative
perspective.

The overall model attains statistical significance (at $p<.01$), and all
relationships are in the direction predicted by the alternative welfare
split perspective. The model has a coefficient of multiple determination
(multiple R) of .367. In short, there is a fair amount of support for the

Figure 6
Path Model Predicting Political Distrust

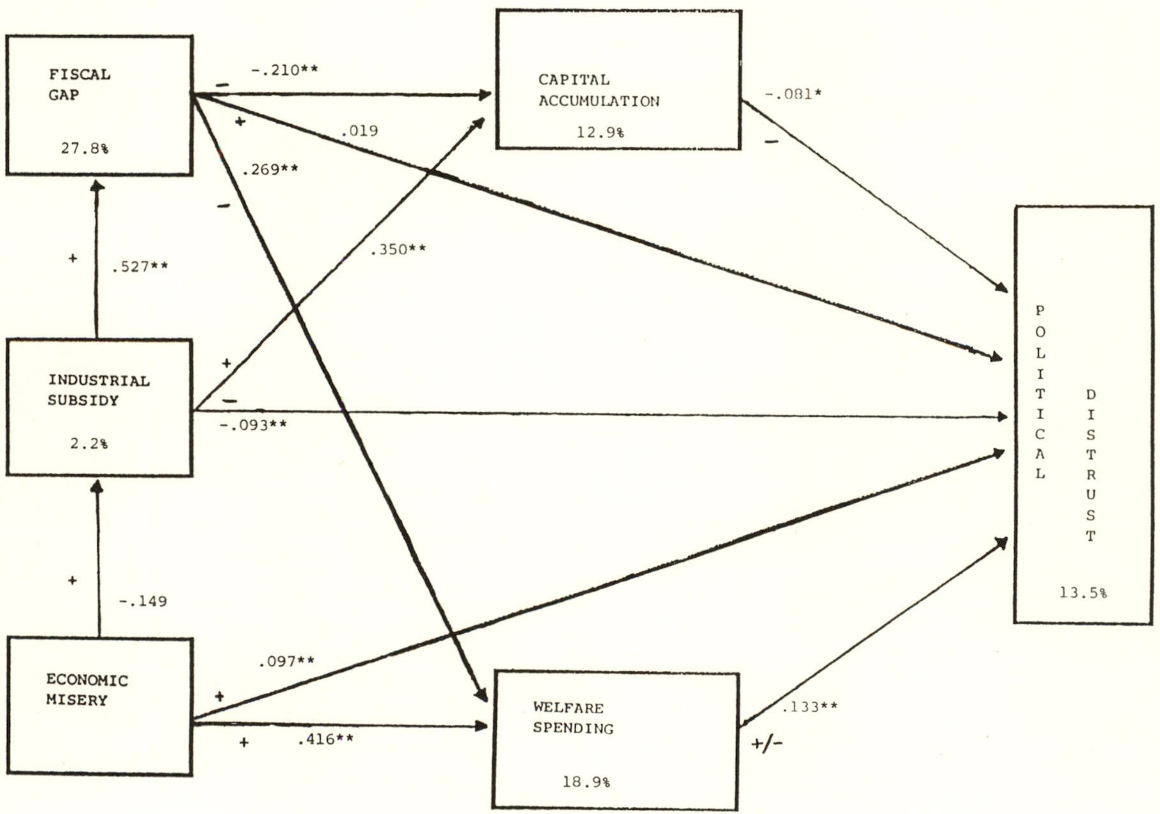

Splitting the Middle

Table 4
Welfare Split Models Predicting Political Distrust by Class Layer, 1964–80

Independent Variables	Capitalist	PMC	New Layer	Working	Poor
Periods					
Period 1968	.083*	.102*	.101**	.149**	.146**
Period 1972	.113*	.172**	.133**	.257**	.159**
Period 1976	.151*	.274**	.176**	.306**	.281**
Period 1980	.387**	.207**	.088**	.347**	-.011
Welfare Split					
Capital Accumulation	-.095*	-.094**	-.084**	.088	-.118*
Economic Misery	.084	.070*	.032	.025	.178**
Welfare Spending	.170**	.150**	-.132*	.036	-.123*
Fiscal Gap	.016	-.012	.001	.090*	-.084*
Industrial Subsidies	-.145**	-.139**	-.012	-.037*	.024
Sociodemographics					
Income	.001	-.088**	-.087**	.007	.034
Education	-.197**	-.026	-.025	-.057**	-.029
Race (Black)	-.033	.028	.018	-.012	-.155**
Sex (Male)	-.020	-.004	-.004	.033*	.050
Party I.D. (Democrat)	-.149*	-.142**	-.078**	-.039	-.103*
Party I.D. (Republican)	-.086	-.117*	-.061**	.032	-.054
Multiple R	.422**	.415**	.418**	.458**	.421**

Source: 1964–1980 American National Election Surveys

*p < .05   **p < .01

alternative perspective and less support for the alienated politics for-mulation.

The welfare split perspective also argues that other factors have effects on political distrust. In particular, it posits that such sociodemographic factors as class position, income, education, race, gender, and political partisanship have effects on levels of political alienation, net of period effects and in addition to the effects of the core welfare split factors. Again, because the focus here is on the class-based changes in political distrust, Table 4 presents the effects of the welfare split variables, period effects, and the sociodemographics on levels of political distrust for each class layer from 1964 through 1980.

Model I of Table 4 presents the relationships between political distrust and the welfare split variables, period effects, and sociodemographics for the capitalist class. This model shows that, among members of the capitalist class, levels of distrust increased at each period from 1964 through 1980. This model also indicates that among capitalists, as capital accumulation tapers off, economic misery increases, welfare spending climbs, and subsidies to industry decrease, levels of distrust increase. These relationships hold true, net of such demographic variables as income, education, race, gender, and political partisanship.

For the most part, the results in Model II parallel those in Model I.

Among members of the professional-managerial class, levels of distrust increased from 1964 through 1976, and declined thereafter. The relationships between political distrust and the central welfare split variables for the PMC also parallel those for capitalists: Decreasing capital accumulation, growing economic misery, rising welfare spending, and reductions in industrial subsidies lead to increments in political distrust.

In contrast to Models I and II, Model III suggests that among members of the new layer, *decreases* in welfare spending bring about higher levels of political distrust. While this relationship is opposite from what occurs among capitalists and the PMC, this finding is consistent with the welfare split thesis. The effects of other factors on political distrust among the new layer are similar to those for the PMC: Distrust generally increased from 1964 through 1976, but declined after 1976 to 1980. Among members of the new layer, decreases in corporate profits generally lead to elevated levels of political distrust. Higher incomes, Democratic party identification, and Republican party identification reduce levels of political distrust among the new layer. No other variables have significant effects on levels of political distrust among this layer.

Model IV discloses that among traditional workers, political distrust climbed continuously from 1964 through 1980. The only welfare split factors that significantly influence political distrust are structural gaps and subsidies to industry. As state indebtedness swells, and as industrial subsidies fall off, levels of distrust among traditional workers climb. Also among these workers, women tend to have higher levels of political distrust than their male counterparts, and progressively higher levels of education produce lower distrust.

Model V shows that levels of political distrust also increased among the poor from 1964 through 1976. For this class layer, welfare spending affects political distrust much as it influences distrust among the new layer. Decreases in welfare spending ushers in higher levels of political distrust. Moreover, lower rates of capital accumulation, spreading economic misery, and growing structural gaps, lead to higher levels of political distrust among the poor. Also, net of other factors, blacks and Democrats who are poor tend to have lower levels of political distrust than nonblacks and non-Democrats.

Generally, these findings provide support for the welfare split thesis. They suggest that factors such as capital accumulation, economic misery, structural gaps, subsidies to industry, and levels of welfare spending not only have effects on levels of political distrust, but also that these factors have differential effects on the various class layers.

CONCLUSIONS

In order to explain the dramatic declines in trust in America's political institutions, it is clear that one needs to take into account a number of the macro-level factors to which neo-Marxian alienated politics theories have pointed. Factors such as spending for social welfare programs, subsidies to industry, and economic misery have clear relationships to levels of trust in America's political institutions. Other factors such as state indebtedness and capital accumulation also appear to influence levels of political alienation directed toward the government. These factors do not influence trust in the government in the manner that most neo-Marxian theories would predict, however. Rather, the findings are much closer to the expectations of an alternative welfare split perspective, which does not posit that the facilitation of accumulation and state legitimacy are mutually exclusive.

The welfare split perspective also pointed out reasons why levels of political alienation should have increased more rapidly among the new layers during the 1960s and 1970s. Results from data analysis supported this hypothesis, net of a number of sociodemographic factors that are related to political alienation.

Despite the fact that state policies had the same deleterious effects on levels of political distrust of the professional-managerial class as they did on those of the new layer, these class fractions did not always respond to their heightened levels of alienation in the same fashion. Indeed, the various class layers often had dissimilar responses to the levels of political alienation that they experienced. The next two chapters will investigate some of the class-differentiated consequences of political alienation.

but did they ??

Chapter Six

Class-Based Reactions to Political Alienation

The previous chapter discussed how increasing polarization over controversial issues gave rise to involvement in social movements and higher levels of political alienation. As noted, there was substantial citizen involvement in "politics by other means," as millions of Americans mobilized in such activities as sit-ins, protest marches, riots, boycotts, and other collective efforts to bring about solutions to national or local problems. At the same time, there were dramatic declines in levels of participation in the formal political process. Because these patterns of political (non)participation took place in the context of declining confidence and trust in elected officials and political institutions, there were disputes about how (and whether) "political alienation" affected political behavior.

Since the mid–1960s, both activism and aquiescence have occurred to some extent; thus, discrepant claims about how political alienation manifests itself persist, and disputes about how the politically alienated react to their disaffection continue. Some political theorists suggest that feelings of political alienation become politicized and lead to outbreaks of social unrest and political activism (e.g., Wolfe 1977). Others argue that political alienation gives rise to undirected cynicism and that the politically alienated merely acquiesce and drop out of the political system (e.g., Easton 1965). Still others argue that political alienation has virtually no behavioral consequences (e.g., Citrin 1974).

To some extent, these conflicting predictions stem from the fact that analysts have not paid sufficient attention to subpopulation variations in recactions to political alienation. Given an American political system in which some groups are denied routine access to policymakers and state managers, it is reasonable to expect that there are differences not only in political alienation, but also in reactions to alienation. To date, however, no study has effectively demonstrated why some segments of the politically alienated population use "unruly" (protest) politics and direct their actions against the political institutions while others abandon political involvement altogether.

Drawing on insights from neo-Marxian theories of politics and "political process" models of collective action, this chapter argues that how people participate politically is a function of their political efficacy and perceptions of the trustworthiness of their political institutions and political representatives. While acknowledging that other aspects of structural location will affect reactions to political alienation, it focuses on social class as a basis for differential reactions to political alienation. It then uses data from the 1976 American National Election Study to determine whether and how: (1) political alienation affects political behavior; (2) social classes differ in their modes of political expression; (3) social classes differ in their reactions to political alienation; and (4) factors identified by proponents of the political process model affect modes of political expression.

NEO-MARXIAN THEORIES OF POLITICS AND THE POLITICAL PROCESS

Neo-Marxian explanations of the political process in America argue that political outcomes are, to a great extent, determined by the ability of various contending and conflicting groups to convince state managers to act in their behalf. Most neo-Marxian theorists suggest that the state has increasingly involved itself in supporting the process of capital accumulation for the capitalist class. As this has proceeded, noncapitalists have ceased to support the actions and policies of the government, elected officials, and even the electoral process. As the citizenry has become more politically alienated from the state, the state itself has become the target of discontent and the object of struggle.

Alan Wolfe (1977), for example, suggests a number of consequences of the state's actions and class-biased policies. Most notable among these is "alienated politics, in which parties and interest groups become responsible for absorbing the common power that people possess and for using this power to rule over the people from whom it came in the first place" (p. 312). This extraction and subsequent reimposition of political power (in an alien form) in turn has the possibility of leading to what Wolfe refers to as "repoliticization."

Repoliticization "is subversive to the dominant tendencies associated with the late capitalist state" (p. 345). Repoliticization involves active attempts by people to re-establish meaningful political activity by exercising strategies that go beyond the formal political arena. "The most compelling form of repoliticization involves the direct expenditure of political power by people on alternatives decided by themselves. Not satisfied with other forms of participation and searching for a vehicle to express their repoliticization, people associate themselves with organized political movements whose purpose is to share social power with people rather than to hold it over them" (p. 345). Such strategies can also be used to complement activities within the electoral system as long as there is a commitment to nonalienated politics. It is repoliticization in the form of activism in both conventional and unconventional political activities that poses the most immediate threat to the late capitalist state; it is this reaction that is most likely to make the contradictions between liberalism and democracy most apparent and, therefore, to call for democratization of the accumulation process. This outcome of alienated politics is especially threatening to the capitalist state when vast numbers of citizens are involved.

While such reactions to alienated politics are possible, they are not necessarily likely, for it is one thing to realize that the political institutions are not serving one's interests and quite another thing to actually engage in activities to rectify such a situation. Piven and Cloward (1977) demonstrate an awareness of this fact in their model of politics in the United States. They argue that "modes of [political] participation, and the degree of influence that result [are] consistently determined by location in the class structure" (p. 3). Starting with the premise that participation in the formal, electoral-representative process is an ineffectual mode of participation for the poor and other subordinated groups, Piven and Cloward argue that protest tactics that defy political norms have been the only recourse for such groups when they have attempted to have their interests furthered via the political arena: "... it is usually when unrest among the lower classes breaks out of the confines of electoral procedures that the poor may have some influence, for the instability and polarization they then threaten to create by their actions ... may force some response from electoral leaders" (p. 15). Yet Piven and Cloward also point out that even protest is not a form of participation that can be pursued at all times or even most times: "The occasions when protest is possible among the poor, the forms that it must take, and the impact it can have are all delimited by the social structure ..." (p. 3); moreover, "only under exceptional conditions are the lower classes afforded the socially determined opportunity to press for their own class interests" (p. 7).

Piven and Cloward argue that protest strategies utilized by the poor are effective political weapons (only) to the extent that they have disruptive effects on the normal operations of institutions. They point out the limitations of such tactics:

(1) [T]he lower classes are often in weak institutional locations to use disruption as a tactic for influence. Many among the lower classes are in locations that make their cooperation less than crucial to the functioning of major institutions. . . . (2) Those who manage the institutions in which many of the lower classes find themselves often have little to concede to disruptors. . . . (3) Finally, lower-class groups have little ability to protect themselves against reprisals that can be employed by institutional managers (p. 25).

More importantly here, Piven and Cloward point out that "the political impact of institutional disruptions depends upon electoral conditions" (p. 31) in that they are ultimately mediated by the electoral-representative system.

In his discussion of "stable unrepresentation," Bill Gamson (1968b, pp. 19–20) points out reasons why, despite the existence of discontented groups that are not having their wants satisfied, objective nonrepresentation does not get translated into actions against the state: "the American political system normally functions to (1) keep unrepresented groups from developing solidarity and politically organizing, and (2) discourage their effective entry into the competitive establishment if and as they become organized." Those groups that are most peripheral and marginal to the American political system are most likely to be discontent and, thus, most likely to distrust the system. However, these are the same groups that are least likely to have a forum or audience to listen to their claims about the state's practices and the least likely to pose a serious threat to the perpetuation of the status quo. Questions about the operation of political institutions need not be taken seriously by authorities to the extent that they are raised by groups denied opportunities to express their discontent.

Along similar lines, Gamson (1968b) attempts to use trust in political institutions to explain the type of influence attempts that contenders will make and the kind of social control responses authorities will make. He posits that there will be congruence between a group's trust orientation and the type of influence it attempts. Particularly relevant here is his discussion of the group that is alienated by political institutions. This kind of group, he argues, "believes either that such institutions put its foes in office or that they are rigged against preferred outcomes regardless of who the incumbents are." (Gamson 1968a, pp. 56–57).

According to Gamson, such alienated solidary groups will rely on constraints (the introduction of new disadvantages) as a means of influence, and authorities will use insulation (limitations on access to necessary resources) as a means of social control over them. Because insulation is the social control mechanism used to suppress demands made by those alienated groups that strongly question the legitimacy of America's political institutions, they are generally the least able to mobilize resources to bring about changes, though they generally have the most reason to advocate changes in the political institutions. Therefore, the most consequential challenges to the state's actions are not likely to be results of the efforts of just those who have been denied access to influence for extended periods of time.

Gamson's discussion presents a very different picture of the conditions under which discontent will give rise to action. He suggests that the most consequential forms of political participation will come not from those who are "locked out," but from those who have traditionally benefited from state activity but are threatened with losing their position.

POLITICAL PROCESS MODELS OF COLLECTIVE ACTION

Political process theories are variants of political interest group explanations. These explanations generally suggest that political orientations and beliefs such as political trust and efficacy grow out of political interests. When political issues, events, or decisions further the (perceived) interests of actors, those actors supposedly feel more politically efficacious, they are more inclined to believe that policy makers are responsive to their will, and they are more likely to view their political institutions and policymakers as trustworthy; that is, they are less politically alienated. Conversely, when policies and events go against actors' political interests, they are more likely to feel politically alienated.

In terms of how people react to feeling politically alienated, proponents of the political process approach posit that it is really a combination of factors that will determine how and whether people will participate in the political process: (1) feeling that the government, political leaders, policymakers, and political institutions are neither trustworthy nor responsive; (2) having such resources as organizational affiliations, money, time, manpower, and know-how; and (3) having opportunities and willingness to act.

Gamson (1968a), for example, put forth what has become known as the "mistrustful-efficacious hypothesis." This hypothesis specifies that it is not the most highly alienated people (i.e., those who lack both political trust and political efficacy) who are most likely to be mobilized politically; rather, it is those people with high political efficacy and low political trust who are most likely to participate politically. In a later formulation, Gamson (1975) pointed out that the degree to which various contending groups have low-cost, routine access to policymakers and others with political clout determines the mode of participation these groups will use. Because some political challengers are denied access to the privileges and advantages routinely available to others, they are often forced to resort to actions that fall outside the formal political process in order to realize their political interests. These political actors will use those tactics that they believe will be most likely to produce the kinds of political policies they favor, even if the tactics are disruptive, unruly, or unconventional. Others who do have routine access have the option of pressing for their interests both inside and outside the formal political arena, and will do so when they believe conditions warrant.

In summary, Gamson (1968a, 1975) and other proponents of the political process formulation predict that: (1) the combination of high efficacy and low trust will increase the likelihood of political participation and that low efficacy and low trust will decrease the likelihood of political participation; (2) modes of political expression will depend on structural location, resources (such as money, know-how, and organizational affiliations), and access to policymakers; and (3) the tactics used by the alienated will depend on their ability and willingness to use various tactics and the (perceived) potential effectiveness of various strategies. The effects of these factors on the political behavior of the politically alienated are examined below.

DISCRETE BEHAVIORAL REACTIONS TO POLITICAL ALIENATION

There are countless specific behaviors that people might engage in as a result of experiencing high levels of political alienation. For example, some people might join "extremist" social movements, while others might write letters to their congressmen, read literature printed by alternative political parties, withhold their votes, campaign more fervently for those who they believe will better serve their political interests, drop out of political activities altogether, or do something completely different. For the most part, such activities can be classified as conventional politics or unconventional politics. Modes of conventional political expression include such activities as registering to vote, voting, writing letters to congressmen, writing letters to editors of newspapers and magazines, and signing petitions. Modes of unconventional political expression include such activities as sit-ins, demonstrations, protests, and other collective efforts to bring about solutions to national or local problems. Of course, the politically alienated can choose to participate in both conventional and unconventional politics, or they can choose to participate in neither type.

Figure 7
Decision Matrix for the Determination of R's Political Response Category

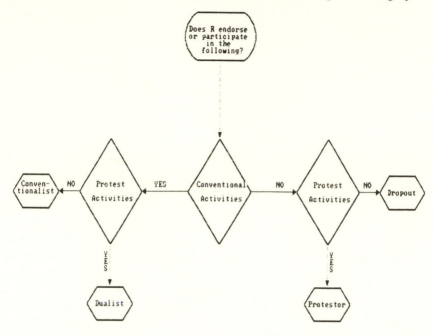

Figure 7 presents a decision matrix that outlines the process used in determining the appropriate classification for respondents. This illustration also summarizes the four types of reactions to political alienation that are possible. This figure cross-classifies (non)participation in conventional politics by (non)participation in unconventional politics. This cross-classification yields four categories: (1) dropouts; (2) conventionalists; (3) dualists; and (4) protestors.

"Dropouts" participate in neither conventional politics nor unconventional politics. They are identified not only by their failure to register and vote, but also by their lack of participation in such conventional political activities as writing letters to congressmen, writing letters to the editors of newspapers or magazines, and signing petitions. They also abstain from participation in such unconventional political activities as sit-ins, demonstrations, protests, and other collective action.

"Conventionalists" continue to participate in the conventional political process (even if they feel that such participation is unfruitful). People in this category do not participate in unconventional politics, however.

"Dualists" participate in conventional politics. They are, however, willing to go outside the bounds of the formal political process and to engage in unconventional political actions as well.

"Protestors" no longer seek results through conventional politics. Rather, they seek to effect desired results through such unconventional tactics as sit-ins, demonstrations, and other forms of collective protest and problem solving.

Proponents of the political process perspective point to the combination of political efficacy and trust, the possession of resources and organizational affiliations, and the willingness and ability to use various tactics as factors that will condition the modes of political expression among the politically alienated.

To measure political efficacy, the Inefficacy index discussed in Chapter 4 was used. Respondents who gave the nonalienated response (i.e., disagreed with both statements) were coded as having high levels of political efficacy; all others were coded as having low efficacy. To operationalize political trust, the Distrust index (also discussed in Chapter 4) was used. Respondents who gave nonalienated responses on both questions were coded as having high levels of political trust. Respondents were further categorized as having low efficacy and low trust, high efficacy and low trust, low efficacy and high trust, or high efficacy and trust.

To test political process hypotheses about the effects of organizational affiliation on behavioral reactions among the politically alienated, respondents were asked: "Do you belong to any organizations or take part in any activities that represent the interests and viewpoints of [the group to which you feel closest]?" Respondents were dichotomized into those who belonged to such organizations versus those who did not belong to organizations.

To measure willingness to use various tactics to bring about change, respondents were asked the following: "Suppose all other methods have failed and a person decides to try to stop the government from going about its usual activities with sit-ins, mass meetings, demonstrations and things like that. Would you approve of that, disapprove, or would it depend on the circumstances?" Respondents were divided into two categories: those who (always) approved of such tactics versus those who did not (always) approve of such tactics. Other variables were operationalized as discussed previously.

CLASS AND RESPONSES TO POLITICAL ALIENATION: A LOOK AT THE EVIDENCE

As mentioned previously, there are still disputes about just how the politically alienated react to their disaffection. Figure 8 presents evidence that suggests that as a group, the politically alienated do differ, to some

Figure 8
Modes of Political Expression by Combinations of Efficacy-Trust

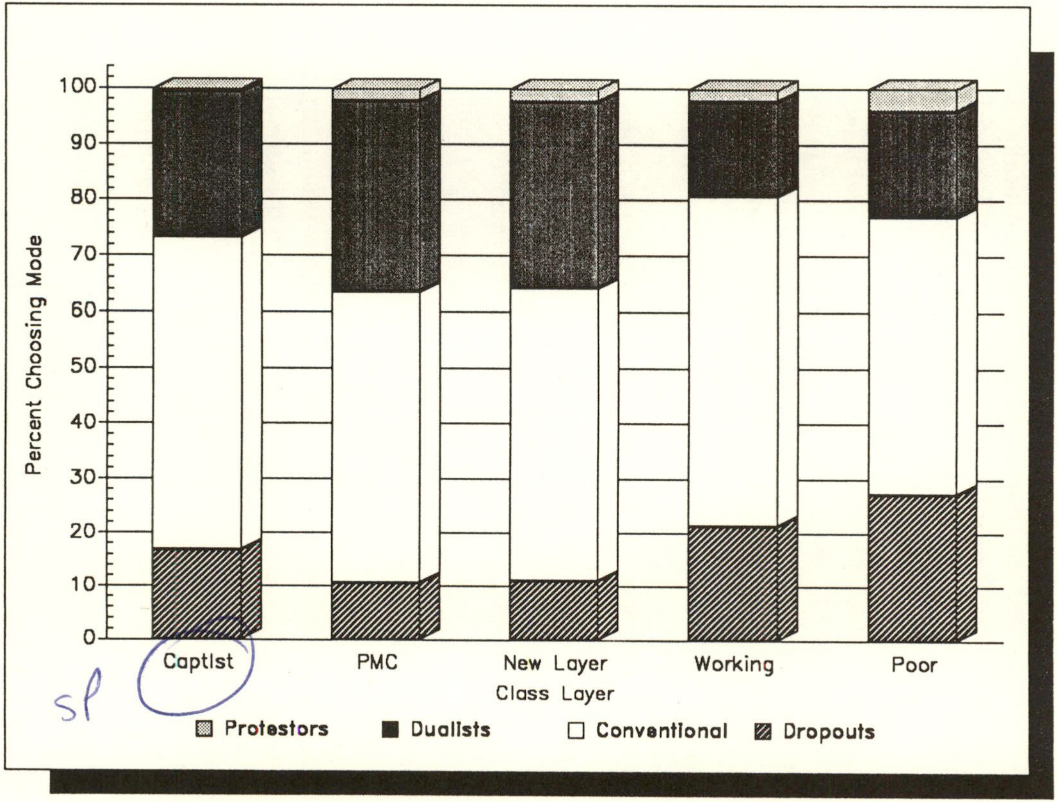

sum — ignores bits that don't fit

not a clear or complete

extent, from the nonalienated in terms of their modes of political expression. For example, a substantially smaller percentage of those nonalienated respondents (i.e., those with high efficacy and high trust) drop out (13%) compared with those with low political efficacy and high trust (24%) and those with low efficacy and low trust (33%). Similarly, while the nonalienated are about as likely as their politically alienated counterparts to engage in conventional activities, and not substantially different in terms of resorting to protest activities, they are more likely than those with low political efficacy to use political dualism (29% verus 15%). Figure 8 also shows that there are some differences among the politically alienated by combinations of efficacy and trust. For example, those respondents with high efficacy and low trust appear to be more similar to the nonalienated than to those with other combinations of efficacy and trust in all modes of political expression. Nevertheless, these differences are statistically significant at p<.01 (X^2 = 58.7; d.f. = 9). Moreover, they are consistent with the expectation that how people participate politically is a function of their efficacy and perceptions of the trustworthiness of their political institutions and representatives.

Figure 9 presents the bivariate relationship between modes of political expression and social class. These results indicate that the classes do, in fact, differ significantly in their modes of political expression. In particular, while about one in ten (10%) of the members of the PMC are political dropouts, more than one in five (21%) of the traditional working class are dropouts, and more than one in four (27%) of the poor participate in neither conventional nor unconventional politics.

Similarly, there are differences among the classes in their tendencies to participate in only the formal political process. Less than half (49%) of the poor choose this form of political expression, while nearly 60 percent of the working class participate only in the formal political process. The new layer, the PMC, and the capitalist class fall between these two extremes, as 53 percent, 52 percent, and 56 percent of these groups, respectively, participate in only conventional political activity. Members of the new layer and the PMC are about twice as likely to engage in political dualism as members of the working class (35% versus 17%). Also, both capitalists and the poor are noticeably less inclined than the new layer and the PMC to be engaged in the simultaneous participation in conventional and unconventional activities, as 26 percent of capitalists and 19 percent of the poor are dualists. Finally, there are also differences among the classes in their willingness to rely solely on unconventional modes of political participation. The poor are about twice as likely as any other group to use protest as their form of political behavior; yet, only 4 percent of the poor are protestors. Less than 1 percent of capitalists rely on protest politics, and about 2 percent of the new layer, the PMC, and the traditional working class do so. Overall, these differences in

Figure 9
Modes of Political Expression by Class

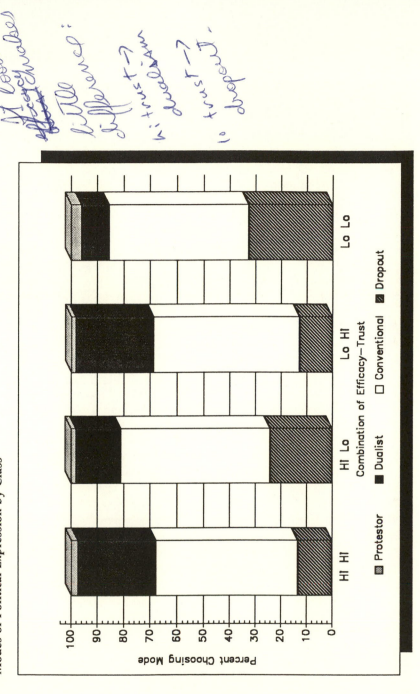

Percent Choosing Mode

Combination of Efficacy–Trust

■ Protestor   ■ Dualist   □ Conventional   ■ Dropout

Splitting the Middle

modes of political expression by class provide substantial support for the idea that one's mode of political expression is related to his or her structural location.

Figure 10 presents relationships that pertain to the issue of whether the new layer and the PMC differ in their reactions to political alienation. This figure summarizes the modes of political expression for each class fraction by combinations of political efficacy and political trust. For each class fraction, there are significant variations in how people with different combinations of political efficacy and trust behave politically. For example, among the PMC, respondents with low efficacy and high trust are more than four times as likely to be political dropouts as are those with high efficacy and high trust, and they are more than eight times more likely than are those with high efficacy and low trust. Similarly, there are differences in the tendency to participate in only the formal political process by combinations of efficacy and trust, as 24 percent more of those in the PMC with low efficacy and high trust (61%) rely only on conventional political participation than do those with low efficacy and low trust (37%). Those with high efficacy and high trust fall between these combinations, as 54 percent of them are political conventionalists. Members of the PMC also differ in the degree to which they rely on the simultaneous use of conventional and unconventional modes of participation, as 14 percent of those with low efficacy and high trust are dualists, compared with 37 percent of those having high efficacy and high trust and 26 percent of those having high efficacy and low trust. The only members of the PMC who are substantially more inclined to rely solely on protest politics are those with low efficacy and low trust.

There are also differences among members of the new layer. These results suggest that for the new layer, they are most likely to be dualists when they have high levels of political efficacy and low levels of trust (50%), and least likely to be dualists when they have low levels of efficacy and trust (12%). In contrast, they are most likely to become protestors (5%) when they have high levels of both types of alienation. They are most likely to be dropouts when they have both low efficacy and high trust (25%). When they have combinations of high efficacy and high trust or low efficacy and low trust, they are most likely to be political conventionalists.

A systematic comparison of members of the new layer and the PMC also reveals some contrasts in reactions to combinations of political efficacy-trust. Although few differences occur between these class fractions when they both experience high levels of political efficacy and high levels of political trust, all other combinations do produce distinctions. For example, when faced with high efficacy and low trust, the PMC is most likely to turn to conventional modes of participation. In contrast,

Figure 10
Differences in New Layer and PMC Reactions to Political Alienation

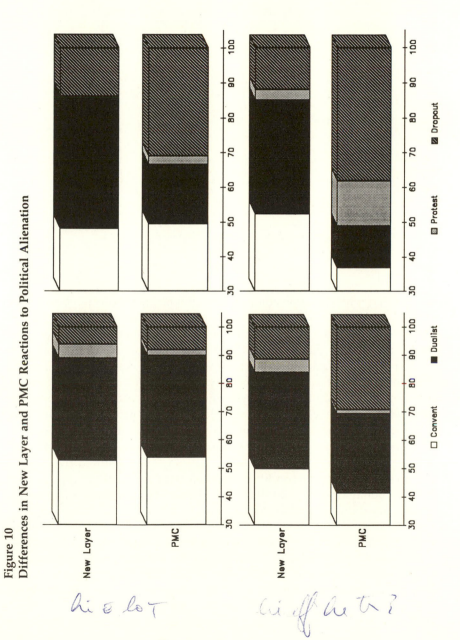

Table 5
Logistic Regression Models Predicting Modes of Political Expression by Class Position, Net of Political Alienation, and Other Characteristics

Independent Variables	Dropout	Conventional	Dualist	Protestor
Class Position				
Capitalist	-.121	.163*	.014	-1.078**
PMC	-.358**	.206*	.033	-.514**
New Layer	-.399*	.191	.136*	-.161
Traditional Working	-.147*	.201**	-.101	-.217*
Poor	.353**	.138**	-.200**	.235**
Efficacy-Trust				
High Ef.- High Trust	-.332**	.188*	.097	.135
Low Ef.- High Trust	-.109	.201*	-.108	.045
High Ef.- Low Trust	-.335**	.187*	.123*	-.011
Other Characteristics				
Race (Black)	-.211*	.117	.013	-.077
Belong	.468**	.174**	.151**	-.003
Disrupt	-.128	-.044	.149	.119
Leftist Ideology	.163	-.307**	.212*	.093
Rightist Ideology	-.451**	.006	.277**	.051
Education	-.067**	.028*	.076**	.095**
Income	-.021**	-.001	.024**	-.014

Source: 1976 American National Election Survey

*p < .05   **p < .01

when faced with the same combination of efficacy-trust, members of the new layer are most likely to engage in political dualism. Similarly, when confronted with low efficacy and low trust, members of the new layer are far more likely than their PMC peers to drop out or to rely solely on protest politics. Under such conditions, they are less likely to use the conventional political process or to pursue dualist strategies. Finally, differences between the new layer and the PMC occur when they feel low political efficacy but have high levels of political trust. The PMC becomes more likely than the new layer to engage in conventional political behavior, but less likely to drop out or to participate as dualists.

Figures 8–10 do not indicate how other factors identified by political process theories might condition the nature of the relationships among political behavior, class position, and efficacy-trust. In order to provide a more rigorous test of these factors and to determine whether and how the relationships are altered when other factors are introduced, Table 5 presents the results from a logistic regression analysis that examined the effects of class position, efficacy-trust, membership in organizations, willingness to use unruly tactics, race, political ideology, education, and income on the various modes of political expression. Overall, these results provide substantial support for the political process model. In particular, net of other factors, class position affects methods of expression as follows: Membership in the capitalist class significantly increases the likelihood that one will be a political conventionalist, but significantly reduces the prospects of dropping out or of participating in protest activities. Membership in the traditional working class increases the chances of being a conventionalist, but decreases the prospects that one will be a protestor. Being a member of the PMC increases the chances that one will choose conventionalism as the mode of political expression, but reduces the possibility that one will engage in protest or drop out of political involvement altogether. Membership in the new layer increases the likelihood of participation as a dualist, but decreases the probability of choosing dropping out as a political option.

For the most part, efficacy-trust affects mode of political expression in a fashion that is consistent with Gamson's (1968a) mistrustful-efficacious hypothesis. Net of other factors, the combination of high efficacy and low trust significantly decreases the likelihood that actors will be political dropouts, and significantly increases the likelihood that they will be conventionalists or dualists. With high efficacy and high trust, the chances of being a dropout decrease, and the likelihood of participating in either conventional or unconventional politics increases. The combination of low efficacy and high trust produces increased odds of being a conventionalist.

Also consistent with political process formulations is the finding that membership in organizations decreases the likelihood that one will be a political dropout. The likelihood that such actors will be conventionalists or dualists, however, increases. Similarly, the willingness to use unruly tactics decreases the chances of being a dropout, but increases the prospects of being a dualist.

In addition to these relationships, the other factors in the model influence the likelihood of the various modes of political expression. For example, blacks are less likely to resort to dropping out, net of the other factors. Those with liberal and progressive ideologies are less likely to be involved in conventional activities, but more likely to be involved as dualists. Those with conservative ideologies are also less likely to drop out and more likely to turn to political dualism. As levels of education increase, the tendency to drop out decreases, the likelihood of participating through conventional means increases, and the chances of being involved as either a dualist or a protestor increase. Finally, income is inversely related to dropping out, but directly proportional to being involved as a political dualist.

This model indicates that the combination of factors that makes it most likely that people will become political dropouts is being poor, having low political efficacy and low political trust, being nonblack, not being involved in any organization, not having a strong ideological position, having a low education, and having low income. People have the highest likelihood of resorting to political conventionalism when they are members of the PMC, low on efficacy but high on trust, affiliated with organizations, not leaning toward the left in their ideological orientation, and highly educated. Dualism is most likely to occur when respondents are from the new layer, highly efficacious but untrusting, members of organizations, noncentrist in ideology, highly educated, and have high income. Finally those people most likely to be involved strictly as protestors are those who are poor and not highly educated.

In short, the results support the idea that how and whether people participate politically is related to their positions in the social structure, their feelings of efficacy and trust, their organizational ties, and their degree of willingness to use various tactics.

DISCUSSION

This chapter reveals the conditions under which people with different class positions, levels of political efficacy, and perceptions of trustworthiness of their political institutions will engage in various types of political behavior. In doing so, the chapter examines whether social classes participate differently and whether the politically alienated behave differently from their nonalienated counterparts. In addition, it sheds light on those factors that lead to differential reactions among these groups by examining the relationships among factors identified by neo-Marxian theories of politics and political process models of collective action.

It is clear from the analysis that, in terms of their modes of political expression, there are differences between the politically alienated and those who are not alienated. In other words, political alienation does, indeed, have behavioral consequences.

It is also clear from the analysis that there are differences among the social classes in their modes of political expression, as well as differences in their reactions to disaffection. As there were substantial variations within the middle layers, the findings are also consistent with the idea that modes of political participation are determined not only by such "objective" factors as location in the social structure, but also by beliefs about the ability to get the political institutions to be responsive, beliefs about the trustworthiness of elected representatives, and willingness to use various tactics and strategies to press for interests.

The results suggest that, to the degree that political alienation resulted in activism, such responses did not reflect political inefficacy but rather distrust of the political institutions and representatives. Also, those responses occurred among people who had organizational ties and affiliations and were carried out by those who were willing and able to use unruly tactics to press for their political interests. When these activists were poor and lacked access to state managers, they pursued their policy preferences outside the formal political arena through the use of the politics of protest; however, when such activists were members of the new layer, they used a double-barreled approach of pursuing their interests through both conventional and unconventional political channels.

It is one thing to say how individuals react to their political alienation, but it is quite another to say what consequences such reactions will have on the stability and viability of the entire political system. The next chapter examines some of the macro-structural consequences of political alienation and the subsequent effects that these outcomes have had on limiting the options of the state.

The specific empirical chapters are loosely linked, like a series of related articles. They vary in the class focus: all classes, or PMC vs new layer. The "split middle" idea is not very convincing — differences are often minor.

Chapter Seven

Some Macro-Level Consequences of Political Alienation

To the degree that political alienation led to apathy and depoliticization, it posed no real consequential threats to the maintenance of the political system. As Chapter 6 demonstrated, however, the combination of low political trust and high political efficacy, especially among members of America's middle layers, facilitated the politicization of discontent. Indeed, such mixtures of political distrust and efficacy increased the tendency for members of the middle layers to become actively involved both inside and outside the formal political arena.

The effects that the increases in political alienation had on modes of political expression were profound and extensive. In many respects, however, these individual-level consequences pale in comparison to the immense changes that occurred in the operation of the political system in the aftermath of sustained periods of heightened political disaffection. With the chipping away of the state's hegemony that accompanied the movements of the 1960s and 1970s, the basis for evaluating the state's performance was transformed, a greater politicization of the state-facilitated accumulation process occurred, middle-layer professionals became more directly involved in social movement and reform efforts, and the management prerogatives of the state came into question when the state increasingly intervened in the economy. Thus, the ability of state managers to manage was undermined and became problematic, as the locus of class struggle moved from the labor process to the state itself.

It is tempting to argue that antistate protest activities will occur when-
ever levels of political alienation are high, disaffection is widespread,
and confidence in the system or a given regime is extremely low. As
Useem and Useem (1979) point out, however, there are problems with
such a thesis. "[T]he translation of grievances into targeted, realistic,
and coherent protest is contingent on other social factors, such as com-
munication networks among the aggrieved and their command over
critical resources" (p. 84). Moreover, without the preexistence of organized movements and groups that can articulate demands on the system,
political alienation will likely find expression in such nonthreatening
forms as dropping out of the political process. Serious challenges to the
state and its operations come from those groups in the society around
whose interests organized protest movements are already active.

When political alienation leads only to undirected cynicism, its overall
effect on the system is close to nil. In contrast, when this disaffection
becomes politicized and is used as a basis for mobilizing the middle
layers against the state, the state apparatus faces serious problems in
maintaining social harmony and ultimately in protecting the interests of
the dominant capitalist class. At the height of protest activities in the
late 1960s and early 1970s, the American state faced such prospects. It
was not until after the demobilization of protest-prone segments of the
population had occurred that high (and still increasing) levels of political
alienation became unproblematic to the maintenance of the system. Prior
to the demobilization of these mass movements, the existence of political
alienation posed a threat not only to how state managers conducted
themselves, the policy outputs of public officials, and the nature of class
relations, but also to the very existence of the political system.

THE CHANGING BASIS FOR EVALUATING THE STATE'S
PERFORMANCE

State managers design and implement public policy. Managers for the
capitalist state attempt to design and implement public policy in such a
way that it will ultimately benefit the capitalist class. At times these
managers do their jobs quite well. At other times, they perform poorly.
In either case, it is quite unlikely that they will receive high marks from
members of the working class for the jobs that they are doing. This is
especially true under conditions of rising political alienation when the
rules of the game are changing and the bases for evaluating the performance of such managers are transformed to the detriment of political
officials and state bureaucrats.

As Lehman (1986, p. 6) points out, "moral approval of the system
(legitimacy) and trust in incumbents (confidence) have been more fused
in the past than they are today." As he notes, "bureaucratization of

modern life entails the uncoupling of individuals and office" (p. 6). The events of the 1960s and 1970s, in conjunction with the rising levels of political alienation, accelerated this uncoupling process. The basis for evaluating the successes of state managers became more rationally based. It became more difficult for political officials and state bureaucrats to garner the support of the middle layers merely on the basis of being loyal patriotic Americans who believed in Mom, apple pie, and other "American values." Rather, these officials became much more account- able for the policies they put in place. They were not as able to tap into the reservoirs of support that the middle layers had previously rendered to incumbents, as the class bias of the state itself became unveiled during this period. Indeed, as the class-based nature of the state's programs became more evident, state managers not only were compelled to design and implement policies that suggested they did not have a procorporate, procapitalist bias, but also at times, they were pressed into demonstrat- ing that they were in favor of progressive programs that promoted the interests of underdog groups and social justice. Needless to say, these standards of evaluation were quite different from those used to assess incumbents prior to the 1960s.

Relatedly, the 1960s and early 1970s were an era of increased demand. This period witnessed the golden age of the welfare state. There were new calls for expanded governmental activity: new antipoverty pro- grams, expanded housing programs, new educational programs, and more safety net programs of all kinds. The dilemma for state managers was that financing these programs was financially costly, inflationary, and did little to appease those who wanted such programs; however, once such programs were put in place, it became very politically costly to attempt to dismantle them, and levels of political alienation and dis- satisfaction with policymakers grew even higher. Thus, state managers found themselves in no-win situations.

To add insult to injury, state managers were often in a quandary as to how they were to pay for inflationary programs that did little to enhance the standing of the public official who had developed them and brought them into existence, and they did virtually nothing to stem the tide of growing political alienation. These officials knew that raising taxes on the citizenry was a sure way of undermining their own support and credibility. Raising taxes on corporations, they believed, would stunt economic growth and development. Even such answers as deficit spend- ing did not seem viable for the long run, and increasingly vanished as solutions to the dilemmas posed by the new constraints placed on the system by increasingly alienated and disgruntled middle layers. Again, these state managers found themselves dealing with new challenges, and they felt themselves being judged by different standards.

Unfortunately for state managers, the increasing demands on the state

state managers ≠ "new" layer?

and problems of financial solvency coincided with declines in their authority and ability to deal effectively with pressing problems. Many
issues of the day seemed intractable and unsolvable within the framework of capitalism. By the beginning of the 1970s, the middle layers
developed expectations that public officials felt were virtually impossible
to meet, and on most occasions, the performances of state managers fell
well short of citizen expectations. Even worse (from the perspective of
state managers), as state activity and involvement expanded, state managers proved even less capable of successfully coping with the demands
placed on them, their levels of authority to deal with such issues were
reduced, and dissatisfaction with their performances became even more
widespread.

Despite continuing claims on the state's resources by the middle layers
and underdog groups, the growth of the welfare state came to an abrupt
end in the mid–1970s, as the onset of economic crises and recessions
placed competing pressures on the state to help restructure and bolster
industry through subsidy and direct aid to municipalities and the private
sector. The state became increasingly involved in mediating the production process, and class conflicts over planning and policy priorities
reappeared. As a result, the state began cutting back on the social welfare
and entitlement programs that it had only recently implemented.

At the same time that most areas of expenditure were being cut back,
the budget continued to grow in certain areas such as defense, aid to
the private sector, and debt interest. What was occurring was not so
much a cut in total state spending as a restructuring in specific directions—namely, *away* from social welfare programs that did not directly
or indirectly benefit industry and *toward* increasing state intervention in
the restructuring of private capital to enable it to respond to recessions
and economic crises.

For example, in 1976 President Ford's budget for fiscal year 1977
sought to drastically curtail the growth of state spending and to reduce
income taxes. His budget proposed to do this by holding down the
growth in outlays to about half of the annual rate in the prior ten years.
He proposed outlays that were to be more than $20 billion lower than
were then-existing service estimates. Also, a major shift in budget priorities was to take place. He proposed substantial increases in real defense
spending at the same time as reductions in real nondefense spending
to reverse the long-term trend toward declines in the proportion of the
budget going toward defense. Similarly, he proposed substantial reductions in several major social programs in health, education, and
community development. These cuts were to be accomplished by re-
placing categorical grants-in-aid with block grants that were to reduce
the overall levels of funding for such programs. Ford also recommended
such changes as permanent *cuts* in individual and corporate income taxes

that amounted to more than $10 billion, with *increases* in social security taxes and unemployment insurance payroll taxes.

By 1978, President Carter was proposing similar budget priorities. The shift from nondefense to defense spending was continued. Instead of making outright cuts in social programs, however, he emphasized increasing the efficiency of welfare programs by consolidating and federalizing such major programs as AFDC. These changes in public expenditures were supposed to help resolve such problems as the trade deficit (by releasing more resources to the private sector for generating more exports), inflation (by allowing for a reduction in tax levels that were fueling inflation), and unemployment (by freeing up more resources for private investment that would stimulate economic growth and jobs). Given that trade deficits, inflation, and unemployment all reached then unacceptable levels, the success of the restructuring attempts for these purposes was dubious at best.

Yet in terms of facilitating the state's accumulation function, these policies were more successful. Acting in the long-term interests of capital, that state sought to restructure the welfare state during these economic crises by bringing about policies to secure a more efficient reproduction of the labor force, by allowing greater social control over the destabilizing groups in society (rather than by trying to placate them), by raising productivity within the social service sector, and by reprivatizing parts of the welfare state. These policies, which O'Connor (1973) refers to as the "social-industrial complex," were used to suit the perceived needs of capital at that time, despite the fact that state managers (e.g., Jimmy Carter) were aware that the capitalist state was in the midst of a "crisis of confidence."

In the absence of highly visible social movement activity, the capitalist state unabashedly promoted the interests of national capital. There were, of course, disagreements among the different representatives of capitalist interests on what their needs were. Various strategies were employed, including some that were in direct opposition to groups who only years earlier were highly mobilized and active. The intent of state managers at that juncture clearly was to implement social policies aimed at aiding and abetting the accumulation of capital. Programs that only met the needs of the poor or the middle layers and did not really help in the reproduction of capital in some direct or indirect way were restructured, cut back, or eliminated altogether.

More and more often, policymakers started depending on the profit-oriented, private sector to provide social services; however, the cost of providing such social services continued to be met by the state. Capitalists were able to socialize their production costs while keeping profits in their own hands. To the degree that this strategy of service delivery was successfully implemented, the needs of the individual, the family, and the community were subordinated to the needs of the market. The society was transformed into a giant market to benefit state-subsidized capitalists. As Braverman argues:

[T]he population no longer relie[d] upon social organization in the forms of family, friends, neighbors, community, elders, children, but with few exceptions ... [went] to market and only to market, not only for food, clothing, and shelter, but also for recreation, amusement, security, for the care of the young, the old, the sick, the handicapped (Braverman 1974, p. 276).

Because these changes in the care of humans were more often to meet the needs of capital than to benefit those who made use of the services, the care for humans became more profit-oriented and more removed from humanistic concerns.

The structural peculiarities of the social-industrial complex (a free-market, profit orientation while receiving funding from the state) made it difficult to separate issues of cost from issues of quality. But the relationship between cost and quality was not necessarily as one would have expected. Because the providers of welfare and social services were generally reimbursed for whatever costs they incurred rather than on the basis of a standard rate, there were neither rewards for cost-efficiency nor penalties for waste. Profit seekers had little incentive to provide a quality of service beyond the minimum that would guarantee them a profit. For many other services outside the social-industrial complex, issues of cost and quality could be resolved in the marketplace; people simply revealed their preferences by how they spent their money. But in the case of state-subsidized services, the providers were not overly dependent on those who made use of their services for their profits. Thus, attempts at restructuring were, to a large extent, successful in serving the immediate needs of capital; however, they also had the effect of repoliticizing the activities of the state and the accumulation process.

REPOLITICIZATION OF ALIENATION AND RENEWED CLASS STRUGGLE

The middle layers are often viewed as a reactionary force in American society. At times, they are. But in the 1970s and early 1980s, with the state's attempts to reprioritize spending in favor of capital to the detriment of the working class, class conflict and struggle were rekindled, and the middle layers again expressed the dual tendencies of reactionaryism and progressivism that constitute their very being. In the absence of progressive social movements, however, middle-layer alienation asserted itself as conservatism. Still, the reactions of the middle layers served to undermine the state's ability to facilitate capital accumulation at their expense.

Class struggle—"the antagonistic, contradictory quality of social relations which comprise the social division of labor" (E. O. Wright 1979,
p. 32)—has been continual, but in the late 1970s it took on a variety of
forms. In the economic realm, it showed up as clashes over share of
profits, wages, and the nature and conditions of the work process. In
the political arena, class struggle emerged as disputes over government
expenditures, taxes, the cost of living, and state policies. In addition, in
the ideological sphere, it was exposed as heated battles over the goals
and direction of social and economic policies.

Most of the history of class struggle between capitalist and workers
can be viewed as a struggle over the conditions of the control of the
labor process. However, in the late 1970s, the rise of the interventionist
state moved the site and focal point of the conflict between capital and
labor from the labor process to the state itself by making taxation and
the social wage the areas of contention.

The forms that the renewed class struggle of the late 1970s took were
delimited by the state and the class structure. By the same token, class
struggle transformed economic relations, and thereby provided the potential for changing the class structure and the operations of the state.

The class structure helped establish the parameters of class struggle
by defining who the combatants were and by setting the range of objectives of class struggle. As E. O. Wright (1979, pp. 102–3) points out,
however, "a given class structure determines only the broadest possible
limits of variation of class struggle. A wide variety of social processes
function as selective forces on class struggle within those limits."

The form of class struggle also depends on the underlying structural
capacities of classes and the organizational arrangements patterned by
those structural capacities:

The form of economic class struggle, for example, is heavily influenced by the
forms of trade unionism (organizational class capacity of the working class at
the economic level). When unions are organized by competing political tendencies (communist unions vs. socialists unions vs. Christian unions), trade unions
struggles are much more likely to be directed at the state and coordinated with
party struggles, rather than simply directed at the immediate capitalists involved
in a conflict. When unions are organized on an industrial basis as in certain
sectors in the United States, on the other hand, union activity is likely to be
much more focused on the immediate employer (E. O. Wright 1979, pp. 102–
3).

In the late 1970s, the most obvious manifestation of class struggle
resulting from political alienation was that of the tax revolts. Because
these revolts mobilized members of the middle layers who were tired
of "big government and government waste," a number of analysts have
portrayed them as "selfish act[s] by [a] hedonistic, middle-class . . . lash-

ing out against the poorer segments of the community who were heavily dependent on government programs" (Rabushka and Ryan 1982, p. 5). Others, commenting on the middle layers' desire for more and better services but lower taxes and smaller government, have characterized middle-layer tax rebels as wanting "something for nothing" (e.g., Sears and Citrin 1982). There was, however, much more behind the tax revolts of the late 1970s and early 1980s.

To the degree that taxation is a coercively imposed set of charges levied on the politically weak by the politically strong in order to finance goods and services to be enjoyed primarily by the latter, the tax revolts of 1978 should be viewed as attempts by the politically dominated middle layers to assert their power. Although the resistance against rising taxes included fiscal conservatives, professionals, home owners, members of the new layer and the traditional working class, and others protecting their economic self-interests, it was not a reactionary movement against the poor. Nor was it an attempt by members of the middle layers to dismantle the social welfare services and entitlement programs offered by the state. Rather, the tax revolt was, ultimately, an anti-capitalist effort directed against the state aimed at shifting the distribution of property tax burdens from the middle layers. The revolts achieved reductions in taxes on the middle layers. Ironically, however, the political climate that resulted from the tax revolts enabled the state again to promote capital accumulation at the expense of workers.

Contrary to popular opinion of the day, there was no rapid increase in taxes in the years immediately preceding the tax revolts of the late 1970s. Government spending grew at a slower rate during the middle and late 1970s than at any other period of the previous decade. Moreover, the share of the gross national product that was attributable to the public sector actually declined between 1975 and 1979. Even more, *property* taxes, which were the driving force behind the overwhelming majority of tax-cut efforts, became a *smaller* percentage of personal income in virtually all states of the union between 1972 and 1980 (Advisory Commission on Intergovernmental Relations 1979).

The biggest change that occurred in the period was in *who* paid taxes. There was, for example, a tendency for residential property owners to pay a larger portion of the overall property tax bill and for industrial and commercial property owners to pay a smaller share. Tax bills paid by individual home owners, consequently, grew much more rapidly than government's total property tax revenues. The proportion of property taxes paid by business declined from 40 percent in 1967 to 12 percent in 1977. Similarly, there was a steady growth in the relative tax burden that fell on workers due to the growing importance of payroll taxes and the increasing rate of "tax exploitation" (J. Miller 1986).

Tax shifts were not the only causes of the taxpayer revolts. Widespread disdain for public officials and beliefs that the government was profligate legitimated attacks on state managers and contributed to the success of tax revolts as a means of demonstrating disapproval of the policies of the state. With the erosion of confidence in the political institutions, there was no reserve of trust and goodwill for political officials to draw on, so state managers faced a hostile climate of opinion as they tried to fend off tax revolts. Declining real incomes and general pessimism about unemployment rates and economic conditions also played significant roles in mobilizing antitax forces. Finally, the sense that taxes were being assessed without correspondingly better services served to propagate the sense that the tax burden shouldered by typical taxpayers was unnecessary and unfair.

Despite their demands for tax relief, those participating in rollback efforts were not calling for reductions in government services to themselves nor to the poor. Indeed, "people want[ed] *more* services, if anything, rather than less. Throughout the period of the tax revolt there was strong public support for larger budgetary commitments on a wide range of domains. This was true . . . throughout the United States, and it was true despite the equally widespread desire for less and smaller government" (Sears and Citrin 1982, p. 47). This was also true, irrespective of how overtaxed people felt they were or how wasteful they felt government was. Even more, the overwhelming majority of citizens said they were willing to accept even higher taxes if they were necessary to preserving existing services, and they were willing to forego tax cuts if it meant a reduction in services or cuts in virtually any social program.

For these reasons it is evident that the tax revolts of the late 1970s and early 1980s were rooted in a progressive populist tradition (although they did include conservative and even reactionary elements). Initially, the middle layers were able to reduce their property tax bills substantially without giving up much in the way of services. State managers were simply forced to find new ways to finance existing programs. Tax revolters were unable, however, to redistribute the tax burden to businesses and the capitalist class.

The revolts did not cripple the state in its attempts to facilitate capital accumulation. Unable to increase revenues from the middle layers, with the election of Ronald Reagan, the national state used the pretext of reduced spending to make more cuts in the social wage and to redirect funds toward military spending. Clearly, the main beneficiaries of these changes were business and the wealthy, as income was redistributed upward. By having their taxes reduced, having the state promote accumulation through its purchase of military hardware, and having the benefits of economic recovery at the expense of working-class people, the capitalist class was successful in this round of its struggle against the proletariat.

Rent control movements were another manifestation of the class strug-gle that accompanied the rises in political alienation and that, to some extent, grew out of the unfulfilled promises of the tax revolts. Although they did not directly threaten the activities of the state as much as the tax revolts did, these class-based actions did seek to change the nature of the relationship between workers and owners via the political ap-paratus. In addition, contests over rent control started dialogues con-cerning which aspects of community life were to be decided by the marketplace and which were to be decided by the community. In doing so, these contests provided the basis for progressive approaches to eco-nomic change in communities.

When renters failed to reap the benefits of property tax cuts promised by leaders of the property tax revolts, fragile coalitions between renters and rentiers collapsed. Few landlords actually passed their tax savings on to their renters. In fact, as demand for housing increased, rents escalated and rental units were increasingly converted into condomi-niums. Feeling betrayed, renters and progressive elements of the prop-erty tax-cutting coalition banned together to push for rent control. Such efforts were particularly successful in such California communities as San Francisco, Los Angeles, Berkeley, and Santa Monica. Moreover, by 1980, 30 percent of that state's rental units were subject to rent control (Rabushka and Ryan 1982).

The rent control movement also started debates about whether rentiers had the license to restrict the political rights of others by denying them membership in communities by raising rents above reasonable, afford-able levels. Progressives argued that market relations were fostering domination by directly and indirectly limiting political membership in communities. Citizenship and the rights and privileges that go along with it, they argued, should not be bought and sold, but should be a matter falling under the auspices of only the polity. In communities, political membership is based on residence. One cannot vote in city elections, for example, without establishing residency: "If the real estate market determines who may or may not reside, forcing current residents to emigrate due to inflated housing costs and opening in-migration only to a wealthy few, then the real estate market has usurped the right of the democratic polity to develop the standards for political membership" (Kann 1986, p. 247).

These arguments, which demonstrated the link between the economic and the political, provided the basis for broadening community reforms. There was renewed discussion about whether other political and human rights should be decided by the marketplace. Progressives in the middle layers argued that job opportunities, access to quality health care, and minimum living standards were also public matters that need not be decided by the market.

Concerns about these and related issues opened the way for the election of socialists and progressives to positions of authority in a number of communities. These middle-layer radicals openly professed their support for economic democracy and redistributive justice. They were swept into office on the basis of platforms that promised to put people before profits. Often, these progressives found a great deal of support for their programs, as they were able to appeal to grassroots activism and populism.

These progressives, though active, visible, and doggedly anticapitalist, posed even less threat to the operation of capitalism than did the tax revolters. Once elected, most of them were more concerned with changing moral values and political outlooks than they were with overhauling the economic system. Other than their efforts with rent control, they did little in concrete terms to bring about democratic control of the marketplace. They did not want to risk alienating other members of the middle layers who were taking a "wait-and-see" attitude toward them and their ideas for governance. In short, these progressive leaders were seldom able to translate their political will into specific, anti-capitalist actions that brought about radical changes in the way businesses operated in their communities.

Another consequence of the struggles that resulted from the extended periods of high political alienation was the tendency toward professionalization of reform efforts. As was argued previously, progressives from the middle layers joined in efforts to bring about social change through their participation in the civil rights movement, the antiwar movement, the women's movement, and the tax revolts. Because many of the middle-layer professionals agreed with the objectives of these movements but not the tactics, they initially contributed financial resources. As time passed, however, they also lent their organizational skills, and at times they provided the reassurance that the state would not resort to overly repressive mechanisms of social control. But these contributions from middle-layer professionals had some costs associated with them. With the active involvement of professionals, the nature of the struggles often changed. The participation of these middle-layer professionals transformed grassroots movements into service agencies for underdog groups, demobilized underdog-group participants, and made the objectives of these movements more cooptable.

Although ostensibly promoting progressive goals and objectives, many of these professional social movements were characterized by full-time staffs, relatively high dependence on funding from sympathetic outside sources and the state, and relatively few actively involved members. Organizational resources became increasingly important to these reforms efforts, and professional reformers became more sophisticated in the techniques that they used to generate such resources. Instead of breeding participatory democracy, however, these movement organizations tended toward oligarchy. Gulfs developed between the professional staff members and the masses that they supposedly represented. Staff members increasingly developed their own agendas and interests. They began to see those whose interests they were supposedly protecting as their "clients," and they started looking to outside groups as the source of their legitimation rather than those movements that they served.

Professional staff members of underdog-group-movement organizations tended to turn to "conscience constituencies" for financial support, as their memberships often lacked the surplus incomes to maintain professionally run organizations. Ultimately, attempts to procure financial support from outside sources served to deradicalize original movement demands and to channel mass insurgency of these groups. The fear of rupturing relations with these conscience constituencies who provided resources often led movement professionals to forswear disruption as a tactic. Hence, professional staffs in social movement organizations tended to play the role of cooling mass insurgency as a way of maintaining the needed flow of resources on which their organizations often became dependent.

So, in a curious kind of a way, increasing levels of political alienation changed the nature and tactics of struggle by getting more middle-layer professionals actively involved in social movement activities and thereby de-radicalizing the aims and strategies of movement efforts.

A final indication of the struggles that grew out of the political alienation of the late 1970s was the renewed challenges to the state's prerogative in disciplining its own employees. In the wake of the tax revolts of the era, there were a number of groups attempting to develop the welfare state in different directions. While these clashes were also bounded by the larger struggle between labor and capital, they also involved "in-fighting" between workers in the public sector and those in the private sector, as public employees resisted the layoffs that resulted from cuts in government spending.

The expansion of the welfare state in the 1960s and early 1970s had created a new and powerful force with a vested interest in the future growth of welfare services. Throughout the 1970s, the salaries and benefits of public employees grew more rapidly than those in the private sector. As budgets for public services froze or shrank, however, these workers were contending for a bigger piece of a smaller pie. The public became increasingly hostile toward the claims of workers in the public sector. The perception was that these employees were overpaid. With the backing of the public, state managers became less sympathetic to the demands of public workers. They tried to make social services more efficient by cutting back on the size of the public workforce and by rationalizing job structures and routinizing the work process.

With such responses from state managers, there was a growing militancy among social service workers. Although the vast majority of these workers are banned from striking, there was a veritable explosion of industrial action in the public sector. There were waves of strikes among teachers, firemen, policemen, postal workers, and other public employees. Even though these were not popularly received by workers in the private sector (not even those who were unionized), they were testament to fact that public employees refused to bear the brunt of public policies that threatened their pay, benefits, and autonomy. Capitalist state demands for greater managerial control and accountability in public services clashed with the ethics of professionals such as teachers, nurses, social workers, and doctors who had developed relatively strong professional associations. So, to some extent, professional employees in the public sector were able to maintain their allodium despite the efforts of state managers.

But professional autonomy and strength also had some harmful effects on public sector professionals in their relationships with others. In addition to the problems with workers in the private sector discussed above, the relatively strong bargaining strength of public sector professionals led to some strains with nonprofessionals within the public sector, as discrepancies in pay, benefits, and autonomy became even greater. Changes in the public workplace fell disproportionately on nonprofessionals. Unions were often pitted against professional associations rather than against state managers to try to maintain resources for their rank and file. Moreover, tactics employed by public sector professionals to secure their benefits were often in direct conflict with the interests of their clients, students, or consumers. Finally, many of their actions undoubtedly had the overall effect of raising the levels of political alienation among other noncapitalists and, ironically, paving the way for even more reactionary political representatives.

descriptive, argumentative, not documented — he ASSERTS the "middle layer" did this + that but does not show they in particular did so

Chapter Eight

The Recent Past and Prospects for the Future

This study began by asking why growing proportions of America's middle layers came to believe that their government, political leaders, policymakers, and political institutions are not responsive to their problems, needs, and interests. Two general approaches that could potentially explain the declines in support for and confidence in the political institutions of the American state were reviewed: political disaffection theories and alienated politics theories.

The first set of explanations—political disaffection theories—pointed to sources of political alienation that are generally political in nature. Three variants within this framework were explicated and empirically tested: the spirit of the times approach, the political personality and culture approach, and the political structure and interest group approach.

The spirit of the times approach argued that trends in political alienation and levels of support for political institutions reflect large-scale changes brought about by historical events that affect the general population in a similar fashion. Thus, this approach posited that changes in levels of political alienation would be uniform among the various classes and class fractions. Empirical investigations of the central claims of this approach did not support them; rather, the results from data analysis indicated that, contrary to this approach's expectations, there were significantly different patterns of change in political alienation for various class fractions since the mid–1960s.

A second political disaffection approach, the political personality and culture approach, claimed that personality and cultural traits explain levels of political alienation and support for political institutions. This approach argued that certain groups are socialized to be alienated from the political system. Because this approach views such socialization as long-enduring, it predicted that levels of political alienation would remain virtually unchanged once sociodemographic characteristics were taken into account. Tests of this approach provided little supportive evidence; in fact, there was substantial negative evidence.

A final political disaffection perspective, the political structure and interest group approach, suggested that political orientations are dynamic and ever-changing in response to politically relevant issues and historical events that have divisive effects in the society. This approach argues that political orientations such as political trust and political efficacy grow out of levels of satisfaction with policy preferences or political events that further one's interests. This approach further specified that political interests usually crystallize around identifiable sociodemographic groups. Though this approach was relatively straightforward in predicting that those groups who believe their interests are not being served will feel most alienated, and that changes in levels of political alienation will vary depending on whose interests are being served during a given period, it did not clearly specify what general type of issues and events would be salient enough to produce changes in levels of political alienation. Nevertheless, results from data analysis were not inconsistent with this approach's predictions that levels of political alienation would differ by class and that changes in these class-specific levels of alienation would vary by historical period.

Another set of explanations of the declines in support for the American state—alienated politics theories—argued that the American state is experiencing problems of legitimacy because it is caught up in the contradictions of the capital accumulation process under liberal democracy. In general, these theories argue that the state facilitates its own problems when it promotes the interests of the capitalist class to the detriment of the interests of noncapitalists. These formulations also predicted that as the level of spending for social welfare programs increases, the level of support for the state's actions would increase, and as the level of capital accumulation increases, support for the capitalist state would decrease. Empirical analysis of the central hypotheses of a general alienated politics model provided support for many of this model's predictions. However, the relationships between industrial subsidies (facilitation of capital accumulation) and support for political institutions of the state were contrary to the expectations of these formulations.

In light of all of these findings, an alternative explanation was proposed. This alternative explanation took into account insights from both the political disaffection approach and the alienated politics approach. More specifically, the state and the role it plays in facilitating the interests of capitalists and hindering the interests of noncapitalists were explored; thus, the role of the state in producing support for its programs, incumbents, and institutions was examined.

It was argued that the state will generally act to support the interests of those groups that have overlapping interests with the capitalist class or those groups that least threaten the interests of the dominant class when only subdominant groups are involved in a conflict. These general tendencies were specified more precisely as being related to polity membership status: members, who possess low-cost and routine access to state managers, and policymakers are more likely to have their policy preferences realized; challengers, who lack such access to policymakers, are less likely to have their preferences realized.

In addition, it was argued that economic stagnation and contraction threaten capitalism; thus, capital accumulation and the expansion of the economy in general provide a basis for state legitimacy rather than detracting from it. This argument suggests that decreases in support for the state would not come so much from those who ordinarily suffer from the economic woes of capitalism, but rather such decreases would be most prominent among those who are more inclined to see the actions of the state as illegitimate when high levels of economic misery and stagnation prevail to the point of affecting the middle layers.

This study also examined the effects of class-based political alienation on modes of individual-level political behavior. Issues addressed included: (1) Whether and how political alienation affects political behavior; (2) whether people from different classes and class fractions differ in their modes of political expression; (3) whether people from different structural locations differ in their *reactions* to political alienation; and (4) whether factors such as class position, access to resources, membership in organizations, willingness to use unruly tactics, and levels of political efficacy and trust affect modes of political expression.

It was clear from the analysis that, in terms of their modes of political expression, there are differences between the politically alienated and those who are not alienated. Political alienation does have behavioral consequences. It was also clear that people from different classes differ in their modes of political expression, as well as in their reactions to disaffection. To the degree that political alienation led to activism, such reactions were reflective not of political apathy or inefficacy, but of political distrust. In addition, those reactions occurred among people with ties to organizations and were carried out by those willing to utilize unconventional political activities. Members of the new layer were more likely than their counterparts from other classes and class fractions to use the double-barreled approach of pursuing their interests through both conventional and unconventional political channels.

This study also examined some of the macro-level effects of political alienation. It was argued that the effects of alienation on the society depend on the political context in which this disaffection occurs. In the late 1960s and early 1970s high levels of political alienation posed severe challenges to the very operation of the state because the alienation was politicized and acted as the basis for mobilizing middle-layer and underdog groups against policies of the state. By the mid to late 1970s high levels of alienation were not as problematic because groups had demobilized and movement activities had become more routinized and professionalized. Nevertheless, the existence of political alienation in American society had the overall effect of politicizing previously taken-for-granted activities and occurrences. The bases for evaluating the activities of the state were changed qualitatively, and the nature of and ground rules for class struggle were altered such that it was now difficult for state managers to use pre–1960s methods to solve the problems they faced.

It is one thing to use empirical data to "predict" the past, but quite another to explain what historical trends portend for the future. This is especially true in the case of political circumstances that are rife with ironies, paradoxes, and contradictions, and is even more problematic when there are indications that patterns are beginning to change. Nevertheless, the challenge of good social science is to capture the essence of phenomena that underlie patterns so that these understandings can be used as the bases for providing meaningful estimates of what will occur. Accordingly, the remainder of this chapter examines more recent trends in political alienation, suggests what levels of alienation the middle layers will attain in the near future, and discusses what these class-based levels of political alienation will mean to prospects for changing the political system.

POLITICAL ALIENATION DURING THE REAGAN YEARS

In the first couple of years of the presidency of Ronald Reagan, levels of political alienation for the middle layers began to subside to some extent. It was tempting to read the relative quietude of the period as a signal that the nearly 20 years of increasing political alienation in American society were finally over, that the legacy of protest and activism from the previous decades had had no long-term effects on the political system, and that corporations and capitalists could revert to their pre–1960s modes of operation. Middle Americans were less likely to feel that their financial situations were worsening. They believed the national economy was improving. In addition, they were optimistic about the future of the economy. But with Reagan's attacks on the welfare state, his attempts to cut back on entitlement programs, his efforts to deregulate business, and his role in facilitating corporate interests through corporate welfare programs, new manifestations of old battle lines resurfaced. Levels of alienation for the poor, blacks, and other underdog groups surged upward. The axes of polarization differed, but again America started dividing into the politically disenfranchised versus the politically incorporated.

Given the two decades of increasing political alienation, the reversal in these trends in the first years of the 1980s should not be minimized. Among members of the middle layers, the first two years of the Reagan presidency marked a return to levels of alienation not experienced since the mid–1970s. These changes suggested that the polarizing effects of such occurrences as the civil rights movement, the women's movement, the antiwar movement, and the tax revolts had dissipated. Still, there were reasons to believe that the declines in political alienation were to be short-lived.

In the short run, Ronald Reagan was able to exploit anti-state sentiments by preaching against big government and by enacting cutbacks in social programs targeted for the poor. Prior to Reagan's presidency, the most pressing economic facts were thought to be high inflation, interest rates, and to some extent, unemployment. To his credit, Reagan was able to reverse the trends. These actions actually enhanced levels of confidence and trust in the political institutions.

To accomplish this rebirth of confidence, however, "Reaganomics" created a new set of problems. Among these challenges were a rising poverty rate. Also, there were new budget and trade deficits the likes of which had never been seen. There was the "bitter medicine" of a devastating recession to combat inflation that disproportionately punished the poor and marginally employed. At the same time, there were cuts in spending for public housing, food stamp programs, and supplemental welfare payments. In short, Reaganomics made it acceptable to resent welfare and other assistance to the poor.

In pursuing bigger reductions that called for sacrifices from members of the middle layers, however, Reagan reached the limits of his ability to boost trust and confidence through cutting programs. New attempts at cutting education programs, social security, farm subsidies, and health programs were extremely unpopular and provided the basis for cleavages about the priorities of government spending. Thus, achieving deeper cuts in acceptable areas became problematic, and attempts to reduce the size and scope of government at the expense of the middle layers had the effect of increasing levels of alienation.

Also with the election of Reagan, a number of right-wing fringe groups

gained visibility, legitimacy, and clout. These social and economic Dar-
winists felt a sense of historical grievance due to the "excesses" of the
1960s and 1970s. They felt that they had been victimized by tragically
foolish actions and conduct during a period of aberration and extreme
social license. They felt that it was their duty to return the country to
its former greatness, strength, and righteousness. This would require a
frontal attack on the "reverse discrimination" brought about by the civil
rights movement, the "offenses against nature" engendered by the
women's movement, the humiliations and betrayals foisted on the nation
by cowardly "peaceniks" and communist traitors, and the immoral actions of proponents of gay rights and abortion. They saw themselves as
a virtuous revolutionary vanguard whose duty it was to purge the system
of its unclean aspects and to restore it to moral health, strength, and
prosperity.

Utilizing state-of-the-art technology in their attempts to turn back the
clock, these zealots perfected direct mail campaigns, massive solicita-
tions, and the identification of single-issue contributors; thus, they were
able to provide substantial financial backing to candidates willing to
recite their catechisms of faith. More importantly, they were able to target
and bring down enemies of their causes. They demonstrated a willingness to pay to have progressives and liberals removed from power. A
number of political representatives, trying to avoid landing up on the
enemy lists of these reactionaries, kowtowed to their demands and facilitated the establishment of the program of the right. With the ascendence of the agenda of the right, levels of political alienation among
new-layer moderates and progressives began to increase. In addition,
the occurrence of another economic recession in 1982 and the politicization of the growing fiscal gap (budget deficit) again caused levels of
alienation among the middle layers to approach those which existed
prior to Reagan's election.

In general, the patterns of change in middle-layer political alienation
during the Reagan years were not inconsistent with the explanation of
changes in alienation presented in the previous chapters. In particular,
Reagan was initially able to reduce levels of alienation among members
of the middle layers by *reducing* spending for social programs. As economic conditions worsened, however, in order to facilitate corporate
profits, Reagan attempted to make even deeper cuts that directly and
adversely affected members of the middle layers so that more funds
could be diverted to the needs of business. Reagan's attempts to energize
industry and to solve economic and fiscal problems at the expense of
the middle layers did not go uncontested. These actions came under
sharp attack. So much controversy was stirred up, in fact, that Reagan
backed down from his new war on the welfare state and chose the route

of expanding the fiscal gap instead. With this new tact, middle-layer alienation leveled off by the end of 1984 to pre–1980 levels.

By the end of the 1980s, the fiscal gap itself had become highly politicized, and the economy again began to stagnate. Indeed, the most prominent element of the legacy of Reaganomics was the budget deficit. Many observers took the October 1987 crash of the stock market as a signal of an impending economic crisis. They argued that the deficit had to be reduced at all political costs. Again, however, state managers were faced with the contradictory demands of accumulation and legitimacy. Given the political context in which these decisions were to be made— during an election year when no viable political leader was willing to call for an increase in taxes, a cut in social spending, nor a reduction of state subsidies to industry—the warning of an economic collapse was to go unheeded. These expedient decisions had the short-run result of maintaining relatively low levels of political alienation. In the longer run, however, when policies to deal with the structural gap have to be implemented in order to ward off the kinds of calamities that occurred in the 1930s, levels of political alienation will be higher than ever.

WHICH WAY AMERICA? MIDDLE-LAYER POLITICAL ALIENATION IN THE POST-REAGAN YEARS

According to such prominent political theorists as James O'Connor (1973) and Alan Wolfe (1977), when it comes to resolving the contradictions of democracy under capitalism that have given rise to the increasingly high levels of political alienation, there are ultimately only two real choices in the long run, neither of which is very attractive to most middle-layer Americans. The state can either: (1) democratize the accumulation process (and thereby prevent nonrepresentative power holders from using the process to suit their own needs); or (2) abandon its pursuit of democracy and relinquish its claims to popular sovereignty.

The first option, democratization of the economic order, would require new forms of class struggle and new movements that are more explicitly linked to class interests. Given that public confidence in business is even lower than that accorded to the political institutions, advances against narrow corporate interests that undermine the public good are possible. Progress in revising the relationship between private property and the public good is also possible, but requires the execution of an educative strategy in which the citizenry gains insights about how corporations unilaterally make policy decisions that affect their lives. Citizens must be given a better understanding of the workings and quasi-governmental powers of private companies. They must be shown that it is their right to have a voice in such corporate bodies, much as they do on regulatory commissions and public utilities. Also, businesses must be castigated for the frequency with which their former executives appear on the boards of regulatory agencies and vice versa. These business elites must be replaced by concerned representatives from the communities affected by the corporate presence. This exchange of personnel will contribute to the establishment of a more democratic order by providing a steady movement of information, orientations, and basic organizational common sense back and forth between the community and the corporate world. Agents of the citizenry will be more able to fulfill their roles as one element in the sorely needed educative process. Without this restructuring and exchange of personnel, battles for economic democracy and against expanding corporatism cannot be successfully waged. Accordingly, ownership of private property must no longer be allowed to be the determining factor in policies that affect communities; rather, a new rationale more deeply rooted in the precepts of democracy must emerge if the clash between corporate interests and community interests is to be settled in favor of the people.

The second option, abandonment of democracy in favor of corporatism and "friendly fascism," would merely require a continuation and extension of Reaganism. In this context, "corporatism" refers to the organization of the society into industrial corporations that serve as agencies of political representation (or in the case of noncapitalists, subordination) and exercise control over policies and activities within their jurisdiction. It represents an even greater concentration of clout in the hands of big business. "Friendly fascism is a new and subtly manipulative form of corporatist serfdom . . . [which is to be distinguished] from the patently vicious corporatism of the classic fascism in the past of Germany, Italy, and Japan" (Gross 1980, p. xi). As Lekachman (1982) points out, Ronald Reagan was the very essence of a friendly fascist: He "must be the nicest president who ever destroyed a union, tried to cut school lunch milk rations from six to four ounces, and compelled families in need of public help to first dispose of household goods in excess of $1,000" (Lekachman 1982, p. 3). Both corporatism and friendly fascism are based on the premise that the political and economic system are extolled because they bring about affluence and that corporate power-mongering is merely a price to be paid for obtaining such goals. But expansion of these tendencies requires more than just prosperity; it also requires the acquiescence of the citizenry. Political opposition and demands for social justice will thwart such reactionary proclivities.

There are a number of indications that the decade ahead is ripe for social change. The capitalist economic system continues to flirt with catastrophe, as recessions occur ever more frequently, last longer, and hurt increasing numbers of people in the society; moreover, stock markets crash seemingly without reasons; world debt (not to mention the interest on that debt) piles up—never to be repaid; industrial manufacturing and production leaves the shores of the United States in search of even more exploitable, lower-waged labor in foreign lands; and workers in this country are increasingly relegated into service sector jobs as handmaidens of the affluent capitalist class. The squeeze on the middle layers continues, and the vice becomes ever tighter. At the same time, the United States becomes an even more class-polarized society. Finally, the society becomes even more unstable, as it increasingly is divided into the "haves" and the "have nots."

The progressive movements of the 1990s will seek more fundamental change. They will, like the movements of the 1960s and early 1970s, provide a severe challenge to America's institutions. Unlike their predecessors, however, these movements will be more class-based in nature, and the attack on capitalism *per se* will be more direct. Because much of capitalism's hegemony has been stripped away, and because much of the justification for the status quo has been chipped away by previous movement activities, future class-based activities will stand a much higher likelihood of succeeding.

Obviously, within the limits dictated by the class structure, the nature of class struggle will also depend on a number of strategic considerations: the groups involved, their targets of influence, their goals, and ultimately such subjective interpretations as whether they believe that they have sufficient expendable resources that can be mobilized to influence outcomes for themselves. How these contenders preparing for class struggle will "know" whether they have sufficient resources to mobilize will be determined, in part, by their perceptions and how familiar they are with the targets of their influence, how acquainted they are with their adversaries and competitors, and how apprised they are of the nature of their own membership and resources.

Contenders from the middle layers will need to form alliances with the poor and other underdog groups. They will need to be familiar with the targets of their influence—the state—in order to better anticipate the actions and reactions of state managers. They will also need to be cognizant of the preferences of these third parties so that they might better estimate how these parties will affect outcomes, whether they will be allies or antagonists, and whether their actions will be consistent for the duration of the challenge. Also, those preparing for struggle will need to determine what strategies and actions will be most cost-effective in achieving their goals with their particular resources. They will also need to know how to communicate their preferences to those who are viewed as legitimate power-holders, but they must also know what can be done to overturn the decisions of those in positions of authority.

Similarly, familiarity with their foes—the capitalist class—will help these new-layer and underdog group partisans determine whether they have adequate resources to attempt influence. As participants in struggle, these actors will need to know the priorities of their capitalist class competitors in order to determine to what extent conflict might be escalated. They will need some general knowledge of the resources at the disposal of capitalists (and how willing they will be to expend these resources) so that they might better anticipate these antagonists' strategies and counter strategies. In short, how new-layer and underdog group partisans will know when they have adequate resources will also depend on their knowledge of the existing and anticipated resources of their competitors.

The combatants in struggle must also be familiar with their constituents and the nature of their own resources in order to determine their adequacy. They must have accurate, up-to-date inventories of existing and potential resources. They must know what resources will be available for what means of influence. Not only must these participants know the amount of their resources, but also they should consider the scope and level of generality, the liquidity, and the content of those resources. In addition, those preparing for class struggle will need to be familiar with the composition of their constituency, how dedicated these group members will be, and how willing they will be to expend their resources for certain goals. They must know the degree to which they can effectively communicate to their membership through existing networks. They must know how susceptible their members will be to social control mechanisms and the efforts of competitors.

In the real world, participants in manifest class struggle never really "know" whether they have adequate resources to mobilize for influence attempts. They therefore base their strategies on subjective interpretations, perceptions, and anticipation of how others will respond. They also base their actions on perceptions of how winnable their struggles are and how likely it is that they will, indeed, be able to effect change.

Erosion in the authority of the capitalist state has made the capitalist class less invincible. Loss of faith in the system has led to cracks in the structure. Political alienation has become so widespread and cynicism so pervasive that the people no longer believe in what they are doing when it comes to ritualistic participation in the political process or cooperation with the dictates of capitalism. Currently, they engage in alienated politics because of what they feel to be constraints imposed on them by outside forces. They see few options available to them. There has been a great loss of authenticity in the social system. This sense of alienation even afflicts those who are relatively privileged by the system. Even the least exploited segments of the middle layers are beginning to realize that they, too, are participating in a system that exploits and robs them of dignity. In the past, they demonstrated that they were willing to engage in strategies necessary for changing the system instead of playing by the very rules that abused them. But somewhere along the line they abandoned these collective political strategies.

What is needed to get beyond alienated politics at this point is for these crucial new-layer actors to realize again that the social structure will remain stable and strong only so long as they continue to participate in it. They must play an active role in changing the rules. They again must be willing to disobey the rules and act collectively to challenge bogus procedures and policies. They cannot acquiesce and must not cooperate.

Given the trends and patterns in political alienation, the 1990s can be a revolutionary decade. Such potential can only be realized through active attempts to force the contradictions of democracy and capitalism to the fore. This will not occur with middle-layer people waiting for the revolution to happen. Members of the middle layers must once again join in at the grassroots with their poor and underdog group brethren to demand greater economic equality and social justice.

quite an editorial as an ending. The "split" in the middle has been forgotten here?

Bibliography

Aberbach, Joel D. 1969. "Alienation and political behavior." *American Political Science Review* 63:86–99.

Abramson, Paul R. 1972. "Political efficacy and political trust among black children: Two explanations." *Journal of Politics* 34:1243–1275.

Abramson, Paul, and Aldrich, John. 1982. "Decline of electoral participation in America." *American Political Science Review* 76: 502–521.

Advisory Commission on Intergovernmental Relations. 1979. *Significant Features of Fiscal Federalism*. Washington: Advisory Commission on Intergovernmental Relations.

Almond, Sidney, and Verba, Gabriel. 1963. *The Civic Culture*. Boston: Little, Brown.

Bennett, W. Lance. 1975. *The Political Mind and the Political Environment: An Investigation of Public Opinion and Political Consciousness*. Lexington, Mass. Lexington Books.

Betz, Michael. 1974. "Riots and welfare: Are they related?" *Social Problems* 21:345–355.

Braverman, Harry. 1974. *Labor and Monopoly Capital*. New York: Monthly Review Press.

Brint, Steven. 1984. " 'New-Class' and cumulative trend explanations of the liberal political attitudes of professionals." *American Journal of Sociology* 90:30–71.

Burawoy, Michael. 1979. *Manufacturing Consent*. Chicago: University of Chicago Press.

Caddell, Patrick. 1979. "Crisis of confidence in a downward spiral." *Public Opinion* 2:2–8.

Campbell, Angus; Converse, Philip E.; and Rodgers, Willard. 1976. *The Quality of American Life: Perceptions, Evaluations, and Satisfactions*. New York: Russell Sage.

Centers, Richard. 1949. *The Psychology of Social Classes*. Princeton, N.J.: Princeton University.

Citrin, Jack. 1974. "Comment: The political relevance of trust in government." *American Political Science Review* 68:973–988.

Cottrell, Allin. 1984. *Social Classes in Marxist Theory*. London: Routledge & Kegan Paul.

Crozier, Michel J.; Huntington, Samuel P.; and Watanuki, Joji. 1975. *The Crisis of Democracy*. New York: New York University Press.

Cutler, Neal E., and Bengtson, Vern L. 1976. "Alienating events: Trends in political alienation reflect historical effects." *Society* 13:43–47.

Domhoff, G. William. 1983. *Who Rules America Now? A View for the '80s*. Englewood Cliffs, N.J.: Prentice Hall.

————. 1979. *The Powers That Be*. New York: Random House.

Easton, David. 1965. *A System Analysis of Political Life*. New York: John Wiley and Sons.

Edelman, Murray J. 1971. *Politics as Symbolic Action: Mass Arousal and Quiescence*. New York: Academic Press.

Edwards, Richard. 1979. *Contested Terrain: The Transformation of the Workplace in the Twentieth Century*. New York: Basic Books.

Ehrenreich, Barbara, and Ehrenreich, John. 1978. "Professional-managerial class." In *Between Labor and Capital*, edited by Pat Walker, pp. 4–45. Boston: South End Press.

Etzioni, Amatai. 1961. *A Comparative Analysis of Complex Organizations*. New York: Free Press.

Finifter, Ada W. 1970. "Dimensions of political alienation." *American Political. Science Review* 64:389–410.

Fraser, John. 1974. "Validating a measure of national political legitimacy." *American Journal of Political Science* 18:117–134.

Gamson, William A. 1975. *Strategy of Social Protest*. Homewood, Ill.: Dorsey Press.

————. 1968a. *Power and Discontent*. Homewood, Ill. Dorsey Press.

————. 1968b. "Stable unrepresentation in American society." *American Behavioral Scientist* 12:15–21.

Gouldner, Alvin. 1979. *Future of Intellectuals and the Rise of the New Class*. New York: Seabury Press.

Grabb, Edward G. 1979. "Working-class authoritarianism and tolerance of out-groups: A reassessment." *Public Opinion Quarterly* 43:36–47.

Gramsci, Antonio. 1971. *Letters From Prison*. Translated by Lynne Lawner. New York: Harper and Row.

Gross, Bertram. 1980. *Friendly Fascism: The New Face of Power in America*. Boston, Mass.: South End Press.

Guest, Avery M. 1974. "Subjective powerlessness in the United States: Some longitudinal trends." *Social Science Quarterly* 54:827–842.

Hamilton, Richard F. 1972. *Class Politics in the United States*. New York: Wiley.

Herring, Cedric. 1987. "Changes in political alienation 1964–1980." *National Journal of Sociology* 1:73–100.

Hibbs, Douglas A.; Rivers, R. Douglas; and Vasilatos, Nicholas. 1982. "The dynamics of political support for American presidents among occupational and partisan groups." *American Journal of Political Science* 26:312–321.

Hodge, Robert, and Treiman, Donald. 1968. "Class identification in the United States." *American Journal of Sociology* 73: 535–547.

House, James S. 1981. "Social structure and personality." In *Sociological Perspectives in Social Psychology*, edited by Morris Rosenberg and Ralph Turner, pp. 525–561. New York: Basic Books.

House, James S., and Mason, William M. 1975. "Political alienation in America, 1952–1968." *American Sociological Review* 40:123–147.

Huntington, Samuel P. 1975. "The United States." In *The Crisis of Democracy*, edited by Michel J. Crozier, Samuel P. Huntington, and Joji Watanuki, pp. 59–118. New York: New York University Press.

————. 1961. *The Common Defense*. New York: Columbia University Press.

Industrial Development. 1982. Atlanta: Conway Publications.

Inter-University Consortium for Political and Social Research. 1981. *The CPS 1980 National Election Study*. Ann Arbor, Mich. Inter-University Consortium for Political and Social Research.

Isaac, Larry, and Kelly, William R. 1981. "Racial insurgency, the state, and welfare expansion: Local and national level evidence from the postwar United States." *American Journal of Sociology* 86:1348–1386.

Iyengar, Shanto. 1980. "Subjective political efficacy as a measure of diffuse support." *Public Opinion Quarterly* 44:249–256.

Jackman, Mary R., and Jackman, Robert W. 1983. *Class Awareness in the United States*. Berkeley, Calif.: University of California Press.

Kann, Mark E. 1986. *Middle Class Radicalism in Santa Monica*. Philadelphia: Temple University Press.

Kluegel, James; Singleton, Royce, Jr.; and Starnes, Charles E. 1977. "Subjective class identification: A multiple indicator approach." *American Sociological Review* 42:599–611.

Knoke, David, and Hout, Michael M. "Social and demographic factors in American political party affiliations, 1952–1972." *American Sociological Review* 39:700–713.

Kohn, Melvin. 1977. *Class and Conformity*. Chicago: University of Chicago Press.

Lehman, Edward W. 1986. "The Crisis of Political Legitimacy: What Is It; Who's Got It; Who Needs It?" Paper presented at the annual meeting of the American Sociological Association in New York, N.Y.

Lekachman, Robert. 1982. *Greed Is Not Enough: Reagonomics*. New York: Pantheon.

Leventman, Paula Goldman. 1981. *Professionals Out of Work*. New York: Free Press.

Levinson, Andrew. 1975. *The Working Class Majority*. New York: Penguin Books.

Lipset, S. M. 1963. *Political Man*. Garden City, N.Y.: Anchor Books.

Lipset, S. M., and Schneider, William. 1983. *Confidence Gap*. New York: Free Press.

Lukacs, Georg. 1971. *History and Class Consciousness*. Translated by Rodney Livingstone. Cambridge, Mass.: MIT Press.

Lukes, Steven. 1967. "Alienation and anomie." *Philpsophy, Politics, and Society*, edited by Peter Laslett and W. G. Runciman, pp. 134–156. Oxford: Basil Blackwell.

Macke, Ann Stratham. 1979. "Trends in aggregate-level political alienation." *Sociological Quarterly* 20:77–87.

Mannheim, Karl. 1940. *Man and Society in an Age of Reconstruction*. London: Kegan, Paul, Trench, and Trubner.

Marcuse, Herbert. 1964. *One Dimensional Man*. Boston: Beacon Press.

Markus, Gregory B. 1979. "The political environment and the dynamics of public attitudes: A panel study." *American Journal of Political Science* 23:338–358.

Marx, Karl. 1977. *Capital*, Vol. I. Introduction by Ernest Mandel. Translated by Ben Fowkes. New York: Vintage.

———. 1973. *Economic and Philosophical Manuscripts of 1844*. Translated by M. Milligan. Edited by D. J. Stuik. London: Lawrence and Wishart, Ltd.

———. 1963. *The Eighteenth Brumaire of Louis Bonaparte*. New York: International Press.

Marx, Karl, and Engels, Friedrich. 1978. *The Communist Manifesto*. New York: Pelican.

Mason, William W.; House, James S.; and Martin, Steven S. 1985. "On the dimensions of political alienation in America." In *Sociological Methodology*, edited by Nancy Brandon Tuma, pp. 111–151. San Francisco: Jossey-Bass.

Miliband, Ralph. 1977. *Marxism and Politics*. New York: Oxford University Press.

———. 1969. *The State in Capitalist Society*. New York: Basic Books.

Miller, Arthur. 1983. "Is confidence rebounding?" *Public Opinion* (June-July): 16–20.

———. 1974. "Political issues and trust in government: 1964–1970." *American Political Science Review* 68:951–972.

Miller, Arthur H.; Raine, Alden S.; and Brown, Thad A. 1976. "Integration and estrangement." *Society* 5:37–42.

Miller, John A. 1986. "The fiscal crisis of the state reconsidered: Two views of the state and the accumulation of capital in the postwar economy." *Review of Radical Political Economics* 18:236–260.

Mills, C. Wright. 1956. *The Power Elite*. New York: Oxford University Press.

———. 1951. *White Collar: The American Middle Classes*. New York: Oxford University Press.

Mirowsky, John, and Ross, Catherine E. 1983. "Paranoia and the structure of powerlessness." *American Sociological Review* 48:228–239.

Molotch, Harvey, and Lester, Marilyn. 1974. "News as purposive behavior: On the strategic use of routine events, accidents, and scandals." *American Sociological Review* 39:101–113.

Noble, David. 1979. "The PMC: A critique." In *Between Labor and Capital*, edited by Pat Walker, pp. 121–142. Boston: South End Press.

O'Connor, James. 1984. *Accumulation Crises*. New York: Basil Blackwell.

———. 1973. *Fiscal Crisis of the State*. New York: St. Martin's Press.

Paige, Jeffery. 1971. "Political orientation and riot participation." *American Sociological Review* 36:801–820.

Piven, Frances F., and Cloward, Richard A. 1988. *Why Americans Don't Vote*. New York: Pantheon.

————. 1977. *Poor People's Movements: Why They Succeed, How They Fail*. New York: Vintage.

————. 1971. *Regulating the Poor*. New York: Pantheon.

Poulantzas, Nicos. 1975. *Classes in Contemporary Capitalism*. London: New Left Books.

Rabushka, Alvin, and Ryan, Pauline. 1982. *Tax Revolt*. Stanford, Calif.: Hoover Institution Press.

Robinson, Richard, and Kelley, Jonathan. 1979. "Class as conceived by Marx and Dahrendorf: Effects on income inequality and politics in the United States and Great Britain." *American Sociological Review* 44:38–58.

Sears, David O., and Citrin, Jack. 1982. *Tax Revolt: Something for Nothing in California*. Cambridge, Mass.: Harvard University Press.

Seeman, Melvin. 1975. "Alienation studies." *Annual Review of Sociology* 1:91–123.

————. 1972. "Alienation and Engagement." In *Human Meaning of Social Change*, edited by Angus Campbell and Philip Converse, p. 467–527. New York: Russell Sage.

————. 1959. "On the meaning of alienation." *American Sociological Review* 24:783–791.

Sigelman, Lee, and Feldman, Stanley. 1983. "Efficacy, mistrust, and political mobilization: A cross-national analysis." *Comparative Political Studies* 16:118–143.

Szyzmanski, Albert. 1978. *The Capitalist State and the Politics of Class*. Cambridge, Mass.: Winthrop Publishers, Inc.

Tilly, Charles. 1978. *From Mobilization to Revolution*. Reading, Mass.: Addison-Wesley Publishing Co.

U.S. Department of Commerce. 1984. Translated data provided by Regional Economic Information System, Bureau of Economic Analysis, Washington, D.C.

U.S. Department of Labor. 1981. *Handbook of Labor Statistics: Bulletin #1705*. Washington, D.C.: U.S. Government Printing Office.

Useem, Bert, and Useem, Michael. 1979. "Government legitimacy and political stability." *Social Forces* 57.

Watts, William and Free, Lloyd, eds. 1973. *State of the Nation*. New York: Universe Books.

Wolfe, Alan. 1977. *Limits of Legitimacy*. New York: Free Press.

————. 1974. "New directions in the Marxist theory of politics." *Politics and Society* 4:131–160.

Wright, Erik Olin. 1985. *Classes*. London: Verso.

————. 1982. "The status of the political in the concept of class structure." *Politics & Society* 11: 321–341.

————. 1979. *Class, Crisis, and the State*. London: Verso.

————. 1978. "Race, class and income inequality." *American Journal of Sociology* 83: 1368–97.

————. 1976. "Class boundaries in advanced capitalist societies." *New Left Review* 98:3–41.

Wright, Erik Olin, and Perrone, Luca. 1977. "Marxist class categories and income inequality." *American Sociological Review* 42: 32–55.

Wright, Erik Olin, and Singelmann, Joachim. 1982. "Proletarianization in the changing American class structure." *Marxist Inquiries: Studies of Labor, Class, and States* (Supplement to *American Journal of Sociology, Vol. 80*), edited by Michael Burawoy and Theda Skocpol, pp. S176–S209. Chicago: University of Chicago Press.

Wright, James D. 1976. *Dissent of the Governed*. New York: Academic Press.

Index

very few non-US scholars, no non-US places

About the Author

CEDRIC HERRING is an Assistant Professor of Sociology at Texas A&M University. He joined the faculty at Texas A&M in 1985 after completing his Ph.D. in sociology at the University of Michigan earlier that same year. In addition, Dr. Herring has been a Ford Foundation Postdoctoral Fellow at the University of Texas at Austin and a Visiting Assistant Professor at Indiana University in Bloomington. He has authored several scholarly articles on social inequality and political issues in such publications as the *Annual Review of Political Science*, the *Journal of Political and Military Sociology*, the *National Journal of Sociology*, and the *Sociological Quarterly*. He has been the recipient of such academic honors as the Spivack Dissertation Award, an American Sociological Association Fellowship, and a CIC Fellowship.